IMAGES

of America

PARK CITY

MAP OF
PARK CITY, TENN.
SCALE: 1 IN. = 200 FT
OFFICE OF
CITY ENGINEER

Chilhowee Park

Burlington

Castle Street

Highland Links Golf Club

Magnolia Avenue

Jackson Avenue (now MLK Jr. Blvd)

Houston Street

Loy Avenue

Sunset Avenue

Mountain View Avenue (now Wimpole)

Williams

Harrison Street

Cherry Street

Chestnut Street

Washington Avenue

Jefferson Avenue

Woodbine Avenue

city limits

East Glenwood Avenue

East Fifth Avenue

Magnolia Avenue

Linden Avenue

Jackson Avenue (now McCalla)

East Vine Avenue (now MLK Jr. Blvd)

East Nelson Street (now Bethel)

Surry

Oddfellow Cemetery

Knox County Cemetery

Confederate Cemetery

Catholic Cemetery

city limits

Thompson Street

Winona Avenue

First Creek (was White's Creek)

East Tenn. Via. & G RR

adjoins the city of Knoxville
at the middle of First Creek

CITY
OF KNOXVILLE

CITY OF MOUNTAIN VIEW
(now Morningside area)

A MAP OF PARK CITY. Park City was incorporated in 1907 as a Tennessee municipality. Park City's western border is the middle of First Creek, just east of the bowery district now known as the Old City. The city's eastern edge, according to a 1914 map of Park City located at the Knox County Archives, is made up of Castle Street, Chilhowee Park, and the town of Burlington. The southern edge of Park City is Nelson Street, now known as Bethel Avenue, and Mountain View Avenue, which is present-day Wimpole Avenue. Chestnut Ridge is the northern border of Park City, which, though corrupted years later by the construction of Interstate 40, still affords a panoramic view of Knoxville and the Great Smoky Mountains beyond, best seen from Adams Street north of Washington. (Derived from 1914 City Engineering Map.)

IMAGES
of America

PARK CITY

Becky French Brewer
and Douglas Stuart McDaniel

ARCADIA
PUBLISHING

Published by Arcadia Publishing
Charleston, South Carolina

Library of Congress Catalog Card Number: 2005931903

For all general information contact Arcadia Publishing at:
Telephone 843-853-2070
Fax 843-853-0044
E-mail sales@arcadiapublishing.com
For customer service and orders:
Toll-Free 1-888-313-2665

Visit us on the Internet at www.arcadiapublishing.com

THE PRIVATE LAKE OF F. C. BEAMAN. Fernando C. Beaman is shown canoeing on the lake at his private estate. Beaman was a forward-thinking man who often seemed to be 50 years ahead of his peers. He created scenic lanes and charming views for his real-estate investors. Chilhowee Park and the surrounding hillsides provided the perfect setting for the lovely homes that Beaman and his partners envisioned. (Marge Beaman Jeffries.)

CONTENTS

ACKNOWLEDGMENTS

A personal note from Becky French Brewer: I grew up on Woodbine Avenue in Park City. I've seen Park City go through many changes over a number years, but I still think of it as my home. Perhaps it is true that "home is where the heart is," and my heart will always be in Park City.

This book is dedicated to all who have lived there and to my parents, Faye and Henry French, who, in 1940, decided to move to Park City.

A special thanks to my coauthor, Doug McDaniel, without whom this book would not have been possible. Doug was already a published author, having written a book about Asheville, North Carolina, and his guidance was therefore critical to me. Also I must thank his wife, Faith, and their son, Jacob, who exhibited great patience when I would call to ask some silly question as they attempted to get Jacob ready for school.

Park City has seen some rough times over the years, but it is still a very desirable place to live. Park City will be 100 years old in 2007, and I think of her as a faded Southern lady who simply needs to powder her cheeks and put on a lovely new dress, and she would be beautiful once again. It is my fervent hope that a new generation of families will discover the charming parks, historic treasures, and beautiful homes that are abundant in Park City. We are planning a fabulous party in 2007 to celebrate 100 years of Park City's history, and you are cordially invited to attend!

A special thanks goes to all those folks who offered their time, photographs, fascinating memories, and constant encouragement during the writing of this book. We hope they are pleased with the finished product. And thanks to Chris Woodhull, city councilman, for offering space at Tribe One on Magnolia Avenue, where Doug and I edited the book.

Each person who provided photographs is credited in the captions. We would also like to acknowledge the following individuals for their valuable contributions. If, due to some oversight on our part, a name fails to appear in the list below, we apologize and will correct it in the second printing: Avon Rollins, Helen Travis, Sara Dee Frazer, Albert Miller, Mike Shoemaker, Hunter Cagle, Lawrence P. Brichetto, Charlie Sterchi, Beverly Gilmer, Vicky Daugherty, Harry McCrea, Harvey Spraul, Naomi Beaman, Helon Brixey, Pat Austin, Peggy Tumblin, Lois Duncan, Tom Evans, Bob Baxter, the Thompson Collection, Sally Polhemus, and Steve Cotham.

INTRODUCTION

This book is about the proud and successful people of Park City. It also includes details about businesses and neighborhoods in the community of Burlington and the town of Mountain View, which was located between Park City and the Tennessee River in the area now known as Morningside. It also includes facts and photographs of life in the area between Central Avenue and First Creek, which was the town of East Knoxville until 1868. In addition, there are relevant stories that connect Park City and its residents to other parts of Knoxville, especially the Fourth and Gill Historic District and downtown Knoxville. There has and always will be an interdependence between the vitality of Park City and these areas.

The origins of Park City began as early as the 1850s with a community known as Shieldstown on the east bank of First Creek. This property was once the Moses White farm, later purchased by John Shields. Another important early landholder was Gen. Joseph A. Mabry II, whose vast farm extended from Mabry Hill on Dandridge Avenue to the land beyond present-day Austin East High School.

From its inception in the 1890s, Park City was home to the elite of Knoxville. It became a vast melting pot of Greek, Swiss, Jewish, African American, German, Italian, and Scotch-Irish entrepreneurs of the late 19th and early 20th centuries.

Cal Johnson, a former slave and resident of Park City, became one of the wealthiest men in the state of Tennessee. Johnson, an owner of racehorses, taverns, and real estate, operated a racetrack in Burlington on the eastern edge of Park City. The half-mile track is still intact as a city street known as Speedway Circle.

Today Park City is a virtual museum of Victorian homes designed by mail-order architect and Park City resident George F. Barber. The first home he designed and built for himself still stands at 1635 Washington Avenue, although he may have lived at several other addresses as well.

From private family collections, the resources of the Mabry Hazen Museum, the Beck Cultural Center, and the McClung Historical Collection, Park City emerges in this photograph narrative that chronicles the area from its pre–Civil War history to its growth into a shining city of progress that hosted important trade expositions of national significance from 1910 to 1913. Park City was annexed into the city of Knoxville in 1917 but retained its cultural and historical identity for many years around Chilhowee Park.

Once a privately owned estate and lake, Chilhowee Park became the social center of Park City, welcoming such notable figures as Teddy Roosevelt, William Jennings Bryan, and Louis Armstrong, to name a few.

While there are many photographs the authors we are able to include, there were other images and stories that must be reserved for another time and place.

One

A City is Born

The first city directory of Knoxville, issued in 1859, lists the residents of two suburban communities adjacent to Knoxville. One was the town of East Knoxville, chartered as a Tennessee municipality three years earlier. The original boundaries of East Knoxville were roughly between Central Avenue and the western bank of First Creek—the area now known as the "Old City." It was annexed by Knoxville in 1868.

The other community on the eastern bank of First Creek was Shieldstown, which was developed on the John Shields farm along Howard Street, just east of First Creek and eastward to Bertrand Street.

Joseph Bell purchased this farmland from Moses White, son of Knoxville's founder James White. John H. Shields purchased the farmland from Bell's heirs sometime in the 1850s. One of Bell's daughters, born in 1810, would marry Irish-born Preston Blang, who would later donate the land for the historically black cemetery, Odfellows Cemetery.

Shields, Blang, and John S. Van Gilder developed homes in the Poplar Springs Addition between Bertrand Street and Olive Street south of Magnolia Avenue. Shields's home was located on First Creek, just north of present-day Linden Avenue near Jessamine Street. More Shieldstown homes were built farther eastward along McCalla Avenue.

Magnolia Avenue did not yet exist, and its predecessor, Park Avenue, only went from Broadway to First Creek. Poplar Springs continued as far north as Briscoe Street, which is now the alley between East Fifth Avenue and Woodbine. With a later Blang addition, Shieldstown would approach Kyle and Olive Streets to the east.

A newspaper clipping about "boy soldiers" from the February 11, 1864, *New Orleans Daily Picayune* sheds a little boyish light on the relationship between "Shieldstowners" and "Knoxvillers:"

> Across a little creek is a place they called Shieldstown. The spirit of war is among the boys of six, eight, and ten years old, and the fight raged fiercely between the Shieldstowners and Knoxvillers. They used slings and Minie balls, which they used with great dexterity. They had camp fires built along in a line. Every morning each party appeared on its own side of the stream, drawn up in array, ammunition was distributed out of a bag, fifteen rounds to the man, and they commenced. Old soldiers of the 9th Corps, who have been through many a storm of shot and shell, kept at a respectable distance as they hurled their Minies with vigor. One day the Shieldstowners made a charge at the single plank that crossed the

stream, the Knoxvillers ran, all except one little fellow about eight years old, who stood at the end of the plank, swearing oaths like Parrott shells, calling them coward; and, by a vigorous discharge of Minies, repulsed the assault. The casualties amounted to bruises and cuts in all parts of the body, rather serious to look at, or to think what they might have been; but every little fellow was proud of his wound. So it went on for several days, when one bright morning, as they were drawn up in full fighting array, and only awaited signal to commence, suddenly appeared some women in rear of each; a half dozen were caught up, severely spanked, and led off. The rest were disconcerted and dispersed.

By the 1860s, Shieldstown found itself in the middle of the Civil War. Mustering grounds for Tennessee Confederate regiments were quartered at the old fair grounds near what is now Chestnut Street. To the southwest, overlooking the river, Fort Huntington Smith and Fort Hill were occupied by the Union Army in the fall of 1863. East Fifth Avenue became the Confederate boundary to the north.

Following the war Shieldstown expanded, as more schools, churches, parks, and homes sprang up. By the 1880s, Shieldstown had grown to over 700 residents in 165 households. The 1880 census lists 104 white families and 61 black or mulatto families, all living side-by-side in the community that would later become the western edge of Park City. By 1869, a "colored" Shieldstown School was located on Howard Street (Linden) near Bertrand Street.

Today there is little left of the original 1850s Shieldstown settlement between Jessamine Street and Bertrand Street except sidewalks and parking lots. Where the Shields house was likely located near First Creek, there are warehouses belonging to a plumbing supply company. The Shieldstown Cemetery can still be found on Linden Avenue just east of Morningside Gardens. Moses H. Lusby is buried there. Lusby was killed with his brother Don, a constable, on August 26, 1882, in a dispute at the Knox County Jail as the sheriff attempted to book the Lusby brothers for brawling. This double murder occurred some months after the murder of Will Mabry, son of Gen. Joseph A. Mabry II, the owner of vast amounts of farmland that were to become Park City. Don Lusby was the prime suspect in the killing of Will Mabry, who was shot in the back down on Front Street December 24, 1881.

THE WILLIAMS RICHARDS HOUSE. This historic home was built in 1842 by John C. J. Williams II in the classic federal style. He was the grandson of Knoxville's founder, James White. John Williams was the great-grandfather of the famous author Tennessee Williams. The home hosted dignitaries such as Pres. Andrew Johnson. In 1899, the home was purchased by John Richards and renamed Colonial Hall. (Mike Whipple/David Dender.)

HORSE-DRAWN DAIRY WAGON. Yellowstone Dairy was located in the Burlington area near Beaman Lake Road and Yellowstone Road and provided freshly delivered milk throughout Park City, Mountain View, and downtown. This horse-drawn wagon was typical of the era. (Marge Beaman Jeffries.)

THE WELCKER FAMILY AT 1502 LINDEN AVENUE, SHIELDSTOWN. Dixie and James Welcker lived in Shieldstown from about 1886 to 1906. This *c.* 1905 picture shows Dixie Welcker and, from left to right, her sons DeWitt, George, Henry, and Frederick. Henry Inman Welcker was a distiller, farmer, lawyer, miner, surveyor, trader, and legislator, and served in the Tennessee House of Representatives (1855–1856) and in the Tennessee Senate (1857–1859.) (Margery Bensey/Jim Welcker.)

M. LICHT'S BOTTLING WORKS. Max Licht came to Knoxville in 1889. He rented a grocery stall at Market Square but discovered that he did better manufacturing condiments such as mustard and ketchup, Big Licht soda pop, Smoky Mountain Chow Chow, and, later, artificial sweetener. M. Licht and Son on North Fifth Avenue has been family-owned since 1889. (Richard M. Licht.)

CANSLER FAMILY REUNION. Hugh Lawson Cansler (third row, at left) and his wife, Laura (third row, second from left), are surrounded by their family. Their son, Charles Warner Cansler, is standing at far left. Laura Ann Scott married Lawson Cansler, a wheelwright and saddle maker from Monroe County. During the Union occupation of Knoxville, Laura received permission from Gen. Ambrose Burnside to teach free blacks. In 1864, she created the first black school in Knoxville. (Beck Center.)

WILLIAM F. YARDLEY. William F. Yardley was one of Tennessee's most outspoken citizens during Reconstruction. He was elected to the Knoxville Board of Aldermen (1872–1873) and the Knox County Court (1876–1882). He stood as a Republican candidate for governor in 1876. In 1872, he became Knoxville's first black lawyer, and he became editor and publisher of Knoxville's first black newspaper, the Knoxville *Examiner*, in 1878. (Beck Center.)

A FIRE IN SHIELDSTOWN. At least eight homes were consumed by the fire when Dean Planters tobacco warehouse on Bell Street burned in 1966. This Shieldstown-era house on Bell Street was one of its victims. There were many Victorian homes in the Shieldstown area that are no longer there due to urban renewal, which destroyed the integrity of that community. (Jerry Duncan.)

HERE COMES THE FIRE DEPARTMENT. The Park City Fire Department races to a fire down Magnolia Avenue in this photograph taken prior to 1915. In the front carriage, the fire chief and his driver would lead a horse-drawn steamer engine to the fire. (Jerry Duncan.)

CHARLES J STAFFORD. Charles J. Stafford owned a farm on Chestnut Ridge and established a public park for the African American community called Chestnut View Park. The park he created in Park City offered one of the most spectacular views of Park City and the Smoky Mountains. (Beck Center.)

WARNER TABERNACLE. Established in 1845 on Fuller Street, Greater Warner AME Zion Church is Knoxville's oldest black church. The church was a stop on the Underground Railroad, as blacks from the Eastport community fled to Kentucky and Ohio. The church was destroyed in 1908 and rebuilt two years later. In 1967, the church moved to Speedway Circle. In 1987, the church purchased the former McCalla Avenue Baptist Church. (Beck Center.)

LET'S GO ON A HAYRIDE. Hayrides were a common recreational activity in Park City, Mountain View, and Burlington in the early 20th century. Local churches and schools would arrange hayrides and picnics for their members, often ending up at one of the local parks, where the group would enjoy roasting hotdogs over an open fire. (Beck Center.)

THE MORNING GLORY GARDEN, SUMMER 1906. The family of William Green Burleson Black (1871–1928) is pictured here. W. G. Black was the youngest of eight children born to Emeline Tillery and Robert Black, a farmer and stonemason. He grew up on a farm near Strawberry Plains. He was a conductor on the Southern Railroad when he built the family's house at 1702 East Fifth Avenue in the Elmwood Park section of Park City. (Margery Bensey.)

16

BLACKBERRY CORNER, c. 1910. In this photograph of the Bensey home, Blackberry Corner, at 1702 East Fifth Avenue, morning glories are climbing on the veranda and fence. On the steps is Dora Black with her two youngest children, Frances and Helen, with her son Claude on the other side. Daughters Annie and Pansy are seen standing with two aunts. (Margery Bensey.)

EAST FIFTH AND BERTRAND. This is the Gail Milligan Sr. home, built between 1910 and 1920 at 1813 East Fifth Avenue at Bertrand Street. The Milligans owned the property on which Park Junior High School was later built. The family had a large garden and raised cattle on the land. (Jerry Duncan/Mrs. Gail Mynatt Ingram.)

JESSAMINE CARBARNS. This photograph shows the old streetcar barns once located on Jessamine Street in Park City. Mules and horses were used to pull the streetcars before they became electrified. The animals wore bells on their harnesses that could be heard tinkling as they made their way along the streets of Park City's neighborhoods. It was a slow and easy way for commuters to travel downtown. (Jerry Duncan.)

ED GODDARD AND FRIEND. Ed Goddard and a friend pose in this *c.* 1900 photograph typical of that era. Goddard was the brother of Cora Goddard Beaman. Ed spent a great deal of time visiting with the Beaman family at their Magnolia Avenue home. This photograph may have been taken at the Conservation Exposition, which was held at Chilhowee Park. (Marge Beaman Jeffries.)

Two

THE MABRYS

Beyond the edges of Shieldstown, Gen. Joseph A. Mabry II owned a vast farm named Mount Rest. The 1840s home still stands today on Martin Luther King Jr. Boulevard. Mabry, the son of Joseph Alexander and Alice Hare (Scott) Mabry, was born in west Knox County in 1826. When Mabry was 12, his father, Joseph A. Mabry Sr., was killed in a knife fight while visiting Alabama. Young Mabry remained on the family estate and was raised by his brother, George Washington Mabry.

On October 12, 1852, Joseph A. Mabry II married Laura Churchwell, a local girl who lived on a large estate in the northeast section of Knoxville. They were the parents of 14 children. Their first home was on Kingston Pike and was named Riverview.

Mabry was a walking contradiction in more ways than one. Although he may be best remembered for his volatile temperament, his contributions to Park City and Mountain View are profound. Much of the area now known as Park City and Mountain View was land once owned by Mabry. His railroad interests, too, contributed greatly to the growth of the area. He was also a devoted husband and loving, generous father. He was a deacon in the Missionary Baptist Church and a Mason. Born into a wealthy and prominent family, he rose to an influential position in social, political, and financial circles. He was known to be kindhearted toward his friends, yet a deadly foe to those who dared oppose him. Neither a perfect saint nor a great sinner, he was rather an extraordinarily powerful man who lived in changing times and yet refused to change with the times.

Mabry was president of the Knoxville and Kentucky Railroad and served as a state lobbyist for railroad interests. In 1853, he and his brother-in-law, William G. Swan, donated the land for a market house on Market Square. Mabry owned and raced some of the finest horses in the South, and it was well known that he enjoyed wagering on the outcome of races. The pre–Civil War years were prosperous ones for General Mabry.

Mabry built his third home in 1858 atop Mabry Hill on Dandridge Avenue. This home, a likely design of Andrew Jackson Downing, afforded a magnificent panoramic view of virtually all of Knoxville and the river.

Mabry donated land for the Confederate Memorial Cemetery and called it "God's Peaceful Acre." The house on Mabry Hill became the headquarters for both Confederate and Union troops. Early in the war, Mabry was a staunch Confederate, making a personal offer to outfit

Confederate soldiers, and in 1861, he established a clothing depot, which provided both clothing and tents. After the war, his railroad went into receivership; he was forced to sell much of his farmland east of Knoxville.

Mabry's achievements were often overshadowed by his outrageous behavior. On June 13, 1870, in a dispute over business and politics, he shot attorney John Baxter in front of the Lamar House on Gay Street. It would not be the last shooting Mabry was involved in.

Sadly the house on Mabry Hill became the site of a double funeral for General Mabry and his son, Joseph A. Mabry III, a young Knoxville attorney. Mark Twain, illustrating the lively Southern culture in small towns like Knoxville in *Life on the Mississippi*, captured the death of Joseph Mabry II and his son, Joseph III, in a shoot out with Thomas O'Connor. This Associated Press telegram of October 19, 1882, included in Twain's book, describes the scene:

> This morning a few minutes after ten o'clock, General Joseph A. Mabry, Thomas O'Connor, and Joseph A. Mabry, Jr., were killed in a shooting affray. The difficulty began yesterday afternoon by General Mabry attacking Major O'Connor and threatening to kill him. This was at the fair grounds, and O'Connor told Mabry that it was not the place to settle their difficulties. Mabry then told O'Connor he should not live. It seems that Mabry was armed and O'Connor was not. The cause of the difficulty was an old feud about the transfer of some property from Mabry to O'Connor. Later in the afternoon Mabry sent word to O'Connor that he would kill him on sight. This morning Major O'Connor was standing in the door of the Mechanics' National Bank, of which he was president. General Mabry and another gentleman walked down Gay Street on the opposite side from the bank. O'Connor stepped into the bank, got a shot gun, took deliberate aim at General Mabry and fired. Mabry fell dead, being shot in the left side. As he fell O'Connor fired again, the shot taking effect in Mabry's thigh. O'Connor then reached into the bank and got another shot gun. About this time Joseph A. Mabry, Jr., son of General Mabry, came rushing down the street, unseen by O'Connor until within forty feet, when the young man fired a pistol, the shot taking effect in O'Connor's right breast, passing through the body near the heart. The instant Mabry shot, O'Connor turned and fired, the load taking effect in young Mabry's right breast and side. Mabry fell pierced with twenty buckshot, and almost instantly O'Connor fell dead without a struggle. Mabry tried to rise, but fell back dead. The whole tragedy occurred within two minutes, and none of the three spoke after he was shot. General Mabry had about thirty buckshot in his body. A bystander was painfully wounded in the thigh with buckshot, and another was wounded in the arm. Four other men had their clothing pierced by buckshot. The affair caused great excitement, and Gay Street was thronged with thousands of people. General Mabry and his son Joe were acquitted only a few days ago of the murder of Moses Lusby and Don Lusby, father and son, whom they killed a few weeks ago. Will Mabry was killed by Don Lusby last Christmas. Major Thomas O'Connor was President of the Mechanics' National Bank here, and was the wealthiest man in the State.

GEN. JOSEPH A. MABRY II. Gen. Joseph A. Mabry II was born April 26, 1826, on a large west Knoxville estate, the son of Joseph A. Mabry Sr. and Alice Scott Hare. His father was killed in an altercation in Alabama when Joseph was only 12 years old. He remained on the estate with his family until he married Laura Churchwell, whose family owned a vast farm in north Knoxville. They were married for 30 years and had 14 children. Mabry was a large landowner, a banker, owner of a newspaper, railroad president, real-estate broker, devotee of horse racing, and lifelong Democrat. In the final years of his life, he began to drink heavily and was prone to fits of anger over the loss of his son Will, who was killed on Christmas Eve, 1881. (Mabry Hazen Museum.)

JOSEPH A. MABRY II AND LAURA CHURCHWELL. Joseph Mabry wed Laura Churchwell, daughter of George and Rebecca Churchwell, October 12, 1852. Springdale, the Churchwell estate, was known for of its magnificent stand of timber. Some of Knoxville's finest homes were built from this timber. Two streets in the Oakwood-Lincoln Park area are named in honor of the family: Churchwell Avenue and Springdale Avenue. (Mabry Hazen Museum.)

A BRIDE'S FIRST HOME. Joseph Mabry presented his bride Laura with this lovely brick home named *Riverview*. The house once stood at the location now occupied by Tyson Junior High School. Laura was never really happy living there and was pleased when their second home was completed. It must have been cleaning day at the Mabry household—notice the rugs hanging over the upper porch railing. (Mabry Hazen Museum.)

ON LOOKOUT MOUNTAIN IN CHATTANOOGA. Gen. Joseph A. Mabry II sits atop a rock on Lookout Mountain in Chattanooga. During the Civil War, he often received letters from prisoners of war asking for help. One letter requested a "small amount" to help buy necessities. On the back of the letter is a notation that $30.00 was sent on July 19, 1864. (Mabry Hazen Museum.)

COLD SPRINGS SUMMER HOME. This was the second home built by General Mabry for his growing family in the 1840s. This home still stands on Martin Luther King Jr. Boulevard. Mabry named this home Mount Rest, but Laura always called it Cold Springs because of the cold water spring a few yards from the house. Many homeowners in Park City will note that Cold Springs subdivision is shown on their deeds. (Mabry Hazen Museum.)

HELMET, SON OF LEXINGTON. Gen. Joseph A. Mabry II owned fine racehorses like this one, named Helmet, sired by the famous racehorse Lexington. Mabry enjoyed attending local horse races, which were held at the South Knoxville fairgrounds and at Cal Johnson's racetrack in Burlington. Mabry developed a friendship with Cal Johnson because he greatly admired Cal's skills with horses and often raced his horses against Johnson's. (Mabry Hazen Museum.)

THE MABRY HAZEN HOUSE. This beautiful pre–Civil War home was the third and last house built by General Mabry for his wife, Laura. This home was constructed in 1858 and was the last home the general would ever occupy. In October 1882, General Mabry and his son Joseph would lie in state in the parlor of this house following their deaths in a violent gun battle on Gay Street. General Mabry's daughter Alice married Rush Strong Hazen. (Mabry Hazen Museum.)

INTERIOR PARLOR OF GENERAL MABRY'S HOUSE. This 1890s photograph shows an interior parlor of the Mabry home on Dandridge Avenue. Notice the magnificent Tennessee marble mantle, which General Mabry had designed especially for this room. He was a great admirer of the local marble, and it can be found in other mantles throughout the home. (Mabry Hazen Museum.)

FRONT PORCH AT MABRY HILL. Laura Mabry (left) and her daughters, Lillian (center), age 3, and Alice, pose for this photograph on Alice's 18th birthday. Alice wrote in her diary that day, April 27, 1874, "It is my birthday, and a more lovely day was never seen. . . . The moon seems brighter than ever before. This evening I have watched, all alone, on the front porch, the stars for hours. . . . I build air castles, never to be realized in the moonlight." (Mabry Hazen Museum.)

KNOXVILLE AND KENTUCKY RAILROAD. General Mabry served as president of the Knoxville and Kentucky Railroad from 1858 to 1864. This railroad was originally chartered in 1852 to answer a great need in East Tennessee. It finally allowed Knoxville to connect to Cincinnati and Charleston, South Carolina. The line was also used to transport valuable coal from Louisville, Kentucky, into the Knoxville market. (Mabry Hazen Museum.)

THE OLD MARKET HOUSE. This picture of the Market House, with Market Square in the foreground, would have pleased General Mabry. Had it not been for his generosity, this public marketplace might not have existed. General Mabry and his brother-in-law, William G. Swan, wanted to invest in the future of Knoxville and donated the land upon which the Market House was built. Although the building is gone, a new generation of forward-thinking citizens is today recapturing the charm and history of Market Square. (Hoskins Library.)

CONFEDERATE MEMORIAL CEMETERY. General Mabry donated the land for this cemetery, having recognized the need for a place to bury Knoxville's fallen soldiers. He hired Cal Johnson, a freed slave, to gather the bodies, which had been hastily buried in other locations, for re-interment here. The confederate soldier atop the monument is the only one in the country who is defiantly facing North. (Mabry Hazen Museum.)

WILL MABRY. William Mabry, youngest son of Gen. Joseph Mabry, died at age 24 following an altercation with Don Lusby on Christmas Eve, 1881. The two had spent the evening drinking and attending a cock fight in the county. Upon returning to Knoxville, an alcohol-related quarrel erupted, and Will was shot twice in the back as he fled from Alf Snodderly's bar on the riverfront. (Mabry Hazen Museum.)

JOSEPH MABRY III. Attorney Joseph Mabry III was killed on Gay Street October 19, 1882, by Thomas O'Connor, president of the Mechanics Bank. Joseph, first-born son of General Mabry, was 27 and unmarried. According to a special edition of the *Knoxville Chronicle* newspaper, he had "a large circle of acquaintances among whom he was well respected" and "he was a man of gentle spirit who would always counsel peace before violence." (Mabry Hazen Museum.)

ALICE MABRY HAZEN. Alice Mabry, 27, married Rush Strong Hazen on January 24, 1883, three months after the death of her father, Gen. Joseph A. Mabry, and brother, Joseph Mabry III. She is shown here wearing a black crepe mourning dress with silk trim and jet beading. She and mother, Laura, were true steel magnolias, having managed two funerals and one wedding within 90 days of each other. From that time on, the home was known as the Mabry Hazen House. (Mabry Hazen Museum.)

THE HAZEN GIRLS.
Alice Mabry Hazen
and Rush Strong Hazen
were the proud parents
of three daughters,
Lillian, Marie, and
Evelyn. Each of these
daughters would attend
the East Tennessee
Female Academy in
Knoxville and finishing
schools in Philadelphia.
The Mabry Hazen
House would become a
mecca of social events
as the young daughters
reached courting age
and began to join
the socially elite of
Knoxville. (Mabry
Hazen Museum.)

INSIDE MABRY AND SWAN'S MARKET HOUSE. This 1930s photograph shows a typical busy day at the Market House in downtown Knoxville. The Market House was built on land donated to the city of Knoxville by Joseph A. Mabry II and William G. Swan in 1853. Mabry then sold 66 lots surrounding the market house for a handsome profit, creating a new business district in downtown Knoxville that still exists today. (Beck Center.)

EVELYN MABRY HAZEN SURVEYS THE RIVER. Evelyn Mabry Hazen looks out over the sweeping vista visible from the front porch of her home. Evelyn, grand-daughter of Gen. Joseph A. Mabry, was the last of the family to occupy the beautiful Mabry Hazen House located on Dandridge Avenue. She remained single all of her life and devoted herself to keeping the family home and history. She was educated in some of the finest finishing schools in the country, and while attending the University of Tennessee, she was chosen Miss Vol by her fellow students. She helped edit the Harbrace College Handbook, a writing guide for students, and was acknowledged for her efforts. Evelyn was a prominent socialite and was active in the community. She was also fond of cats and kept several in her home at all times. In 1987, Evelyn accidentally fell down the stairs at the Mabry home, and she never fully recovered from the accident. Realizing she might not recover, she established a trust to create the Mabry Hazen Museum and died several months later. (Mabry Hazen Museum.)

Three

THE GROWTH OF
PARK CITY

Three great-grandsons of James White, the founder of Knoxville, and his wife, Mary Lawson White, lived in Park City. James Park White and his wife, Juliet, lived at 1520 Magnolia Avenue, while Andrew Park White, his wife, Harriet, and George McNutt White Jr. lived at 1511 East Fifth Avenue. Their grandparents Moses and Isabella White had a farm on White's Creek, later known as First Creek, in what later became Shieldstown.

Around 1890, the Edgewood Land and Improvement Company began to subdivide lots in the Washington Avenue Addition along Washington and Jefferson Avenues below Chestnut Ridge, east of Winona. The company was also busy developing residential areas in Fountain City north of Knoxville. Some of these investors were also involved in the earlier development of the Fourth and Gill neighborhood.

George F. Barber, a noted architect who moved to Knoxville in 1888, established an office with Martin Parmalee in the French and Roberts Building downtown. Barber and Parmalee were involved with the Edgewood Land and Improvement Company, and they designed many of the homes built in Edgewood.

Barber designed and marketed mail-order house plans, published numerous periodicals, and even maintained his own publishing company, The American Home Publishing Company, which he established in 1898. Barber maintained his architectural firm and designed and published house plans until his death in 1917. His designs were sold nationally and even internationally.

Barber's publications include *The Cottage Souvenir* (1891), *Cottage Souvenir No. 2* (1892), *New Model Dwellings and How Best to Build Them* (1894), *Artistic Homes* (1895), *Art in Architecture* (1902–1903), and *Modern Dwellings* (1901–1907). *American Homes*, which was an illustrated monthly magazine published by The American Homes Publishing Company, continued for six years. If any of these publications inspired the purchase of homes or designs by Barber, a client could fill out a questionnaire and send it with the appropriate fee to Barber's Knoxville offices. Plans, elevations, working drawings, a bill of materials or even pre-manufactured architectural details for the house could be purchased in this manner.

For fans of Barber's architecture, it is interesting to note which homes he lived in according to the city directories. Barber lived at 1635 Washington Avenue from 1890 until 1897, when he moved to the home at 1723 Coleman Avenue, known today as Glenwood Avenue. His first home on Washington Avenue became a boardinghouse for draftsmen working for Barber's architecture firm. Barber lived on Coleman until 1900, when he appears at 1709 Washington Avenue. In 1901, he lived at 1711 Washington Avenue. From 1903 to 1912, Barber lived at 1715 Washington Avenue, where his son, Charles I. Barber, who would later begin the firm of Barber and Curry, also boarded. By 1913, nearing the end of the Gilded Age and the last of the national expositions in Park City, Barber lived at 1701 Coleman Avenue, where he died around 1915. In 1913, Charles I. Barber had started his own firm and was living on Tazewell Pike.

Fernando Cortes Beaman, born in 1836 in Malone, New York, married Mary Jane Sherrod from Strawberry Plains in 1864. She was 18, and he was a 32-year-old college professor. The Beamans, who were living in the Thorn Grove community, moved to their new homestead and dairy farm in April 1876. Beaman had come from New York and taught at the Rocky Springs Academy in 1866. He also taught at Huckleberry Springs (10 miles east of Knoxville), Lyons Creek, Cedar Grove (in Jefferson County), and at Thorn Grove (where he boarded students at his home).

On December 31, 1875, Beaman, his brother, Orin, and Charles A. Burke of Malone, New York, purchased approximately 1,100 acres at a chancery court sale. This property was owned by the family of Alexander McMillan, who had earned a land grant for his military services in the American Revolution.

Even after the purchase of the dairy farm, Beaman continued to teach, leaving the family to tend the farm while he was away teaching Greek language and English literature at East Tennessee Wesleyan College in Athens, Tennessee, from 1881 to 1883. In 1882, Mary Jane Sherrod Beaman was running the dairy farm while taking care of her children ages 1, 4, 6, 9, 11, 13, and a newborn child. Mary Jane died in 1901; Beaman died in 1911.

In 1885, Beaman conceived the idea of a pleasure park on the grounds of his large dairy farm. In the spring of 1888, he built a 12-room house at the entrance of Chilhowee Park. One of the first structures built was a dancing pavilion. The marble bandstand would be built in 1910 for the Appalachian Exposition. In 1889, Beaman made arrangements with William G. McAdoo to extend the electric streetcar line from Morgan Street, near First Creek, all the way to Chilhowee Park, an act that would set the stage for much of the possible residential development in what was to become Park City. Also in 1889, Beaman's lake was renamed Lake Ottossee, a contraction of "the lake you ought to see."

ALL ABOARD OLD #23. An electrified streetcar runs on East Fifth Avenue around 1898 or 1899. Streetcars of that era carried both passengers and U.S. mail. Conductors knew their passengers so well that they would actually wait for a few moments if one of their regular travelers was running a bit late on a snowy day. (Hoskins Library.)

THE JOSEPH JAQUES HOME. This beautiful home, at the present site of Knoxville High School, was owned by British-born industrialist Joseph Jaques. Jaques operated three steamboats on the Tennessee River: the *Loudon*, the *Tennessee*, and the *Knoxville*. He was elected mayor of Knoxville in 1858 and 1878; became vice-president and general superintendent of the East Tennessee, Virginia, and Georgia Railroad; and was president of the East Tennessee National Bank. (Mabry Hazen Museum.)

THE BRANNER MANSION. This lovely home once belonged to Mrs. Magnolia Branner. When Mrs. Branner lived here, the street was known as Park Avenue. After her son, Bryan, became mayor, the street was renamed Magnolia Avenue in her honor. The home later became Knoxville Catholic High School (KCHS). KCHS would build a new building on the site, which today houses Pellissippi State Community College. (Mabry Hazen Museum.)

THE ARCHITECTS OF PARK CITY. A. B. Baumann, the owner of Baumann Brother Architects, lived in this home at 840 North Fourth Avenue. His brother and partner, Joseph F. Baumann, lived at 809 North Third Avenue. Baumann and Baumann designed Knoxville High School, Park City Library, many churches and schools in Knoxville, and many homes in Park City, including the Branner home located at 1724 Magnolia Avenue. (Mabry Hazen Museum.)

WOODWARD MANSION. The Nathaniel Woodward home was built on Castle Hill in 1890. Woodward was a route agent with the Southern Express Company. Charles Wayland, a traveling salesman with the Cowan McClung Company and the Daniel Briscoe Company, purchased the 16-room home in 1923, moving from 2133 Magnolia Avenue. It was a tragic loss when this home was demolished by the Knoxville Zoo. (Mabry Hazen Museum.)

THE MANOR HOUSES OF WASHINGTON AVENUE. This streetscape of Washington Avenue *c.* 1894 depicts one of the more affluent sections of Park City. George F. Barber and Martin Parmlee designed many homes on Washington Avenue and elsewhere. The home at 1635 Washington Avenue, which later became housing for Barber's draftsmen, is visible on the left side of the street. Barber-designed homes in other parts of the country appraise for over $1 million. (Mabry Hazen Museum.)

MCARTHUR HOME IN EDGEWOOD. This elaborate home designed by George F. Barber was built for Frederick E. McArthur around 1890 at 1701 Jefferson Avenue. McArthur owned McArthur's Music House on Gay Street, selling pianos, organs, and other musical instruments. The home, while having lost some of its original splendor, is greatly endangered, but could be a show place if purchased by preservation-minded homeowners. (Charles M. Reeves.)

ORNATE VICTORIAN IN PARK CITY. This Barber-designed home was built in 1890 for David J. Egleston, secretary/treasurer of the East Tennessee Hedge Company and Field Seeds. Egleston's seed business was located on Jackson Avenue near Gay Street. Unfortunately Egleston died on July 10, 1890. His widow lived there briefly before the house changed hands. (Charles M. Reeves.)

A PARLOR IN ELMWOOD PARK, WINTER 1909. Green Black built the house that still stands at 1702 East Fifth Avenue in the Elmwood Park Addition in 1909. The family farmed and raised vegetables on the land around the house. Seated from left to right are Mary Day (wife of William Day), Dora Day Black (holding baby Helen), and Green Black (holding Frances); standing are William Day (brother of Dora Day Black), Pansy, Anna, and Claude. (Margery Bensey.)

J. T. PICKELL'S STORE. J. T. Pickell owned this general store on the corner of Bertrand Street and Howard Street near Shieldstown Cemetery. The address of the store was 1901 Howard Street, and there was a branch store at 1618–1620 East Vine Avenue. (Margery Bensey.)

Cal Johnson. In 1922, Cal Johnson commissioned the design for this grand archway for the entrance to the park named in his honor. The original address of the park was 225 East Clinch Avenue. G. F. Johnson was the general manager of the park. Cal Johnson and his wife, Maggie, lived at 317 State Street. He was married three times, but none of these marriages produced children. Johnson once worked as a bartender and cook but quickly developed an acumen for real estate, horses, taverns, and saloons. An extremely wealthy man, Johnson owned racetracks at Speedway Circle in Burlington and in south Knoxville. When Johnson died, he was reported to be one of the wealthiest men in Tennessee. Today the beautiful fountain and elegant marble archway are missing from Cal Johnson Park, now 507 Hall of Fame Drive. Their whereabouts are unknown. (Beck Center.)

FIRST AEROPLANE IN KNOXVILLE. This photograph was taken in 1911 at Speedway Circle, when the first airplane landed in Knoxville. Cal Johnson, owner of Speedway Circle Race Track, reluctantly cut down the only tree that stood inside the center of the track in order to provide enough space for the plane to safely land. (Ernie, Bob, and Debbie Barnes.)

MAYOR OF PARK CITY. William Alexander Davis was born in Knoxville in 1862. He went to work as a depot master for the Southern Railway in 1890. A charter member of the Park City Council in 1907, he served four terms before serving two terms as Park City mayor. He later served two terms on Knoxville City Council. He and his wife, Cora Pope Davis, attended Fifth Avenue Presbyterian Church. (Lillian Mashburn.)

39

A DREAM IS BORN. Clarence Beaman Sr. is pictured here with several of his friends at the 1897 Toronto World's Fair. Perhaps it was at this very pavilion that the idea for the Appalachian Conservation Exposition, which was held at Chilhowee Park in 1910, was first born. Dreaming big like his father, F. C. Beaman, Clarence made the dream of an exposition at the park a reality within a few short years. (Marge Beaman Jeffries.)

HEADED TO THE EXPOSITION. Chilhowee Park was the hub of social activity for Park City and Knoxville proper, and it kept the streetcars busy hauling passengers from downtown to Chilhowee Park. In 1889, F. C. Beaman knew that the future of his park would depend upon public transportation, so he persevered until a streetcar made its first round trip to the park on May 1, 1890. (Thompson Photo.)

Four

THERE ARE PARKS IN PARK CITY

Park City has always had visionary leaders who believed in the importance and desirability of quiet, shaded green spaces nestled within the residential sections, available for public use.

Streetcar development would prove critical to the success of Chilhowee Park and Park City. When the streetcar line was completed to Chilhowee Park, people in Knoxville could jump on a streetcar and quickly reach the distant park. William G. McAdoo commuted almost daily between Chattanooga and Knoxville—a distance of 120 miles—to personally supervise construction. On May 1, 1890, the first electric streetcar ran from Gay Street to Lake Ottossee.

As McAdoo built the Magnolia streetcar line in 1896, his Citizens Street Railway Company leased the Lake Ottossee property, but the lake reverted to Beaman when that company liquidated. Beaman then sold it to the Knoxville Lake Park Springs Company, which owned it throughout the national expositions. It was rechristened Chilhowee Park by 1910.

Chilhowee Park would become very important in the history of Knoxville, as a group of Knoxville business leaders envisioned the world's first conservation exposition. They included W. J. Oliver, George E. Helm, W. J. Savage, C. B. Atkin, Rush Strong Hazen, and leading women of the day, including Mrs. Edward T. Sanford (Lutie) and Mary Boyce Temple, to name a few. It was more than Knoxville's first big fair—a national event, Pres. William Howard Taft symbolically pressed a telegraph button in Beverly, Massachusetts, that rang a bell at Chilhowee Park and turned the lights on at the fair for the 1910 Appalachian Exposition. Former president Teddy Roosevelt, a friend of Oliver's, attended. President Taft attended the second exposition, arriving in Knoxville on November 11, 1911, and climbing the hill to the top of Chilhowee Park. The National Conservation Exposition would be held in 1913 at Chilhowee Park, meaning that three national expositions were held at Chilhowee Park within the span of four years.

Some younger Knoxvillians have memories of the 1982 Knoxville World's Fair, but one can only imagine the significance of a national exposition in rural east Tennessee in 1910. A shining city of progress was built, nestled among the hills and waters of Chilhowee Park. As Knoxville would not annex Park City until 1917, Park City actually hosted three major national expositions 72 years before Knoxville hosted the World's Fair in 1982.

Around 1920, Col. J. G. Sterchi acquired the park and streetcar lines and leased the park to the East Tennessee Division Fair. While briefly renamed Sterchi Park, the name Chilhowee Park returned, and it has been home to the Tennessee Valley Fair, golden gloves boxing, and other recreational events for over 90 years.

Lake Ottosee would not be the only lake and dairy farm that Beaman would develop in east Knoxville. Beaman, connected also with Yellowstone Dairy, purchased a portion of Idlehour, James P. McDonald's 1,200-acre farm, and built Beaman Lake. This secluded lake was south of Skyline Drive between Beaman Lake Road and Yellowstone Road.

This lake would later become a problem for the city of Knoxville. In the 1980s, local residents, concerned about mosquitoes and storm-water control, petitioned local government to breach the dam and fill in the lake. Why the city ever let homes be constructed downstream from a dam is unknown, but the lake no longer exists, and the homes now overlook an overgrown wooded area rather than a scenic lake.

There are many other parks around Park City, and others that have since disappeared. Chestnut View Park sat atop Chestnut Ridge and was owned by Charles Stafford, an African American farmer. It would now be in the middle of Interstate 40, west of Cherry Street.

One of the more disappointing losses has been the slow loss of Cal Johnson Park. Developed in the 1920s as a tribute to its successful namesake, the elegant marble fountain and entrance monument have been removed from the park, and the park itself has been reduced to a mere four acres. The Cal Johnson Recreation Center building and two tennis courts are all that is left of what was once a lovely park.

Parkridge Park is a small pocket park on the east side of Bertrand Street across from Old Park Junior High School. The school was converted into charming condominiums several years ago. Neighborhood events are often held in this pocket park.

Caswell Park and Evans-Collins Field on Winona Street were renovated in the early 21st century and have added new life to the Parkridge community of Park City. This beautiful athletic park, the adjacent little-league ball fields, and kids park make a welcome addition to the community. Evans-Collins Field was named in honor of W. E. Evans, principal of Knoxville High School, and Wilson Collins, who was the Knoxville High School's head football coach and athletic director until 1940.

Howell Nurseries, a 200-year-old plant nursery on the edge of Park City at 2743 Wimpole Street dating back to 1786 , is being converted into the Knoxville Botanical Gardens and Arboretum with winding walkways and charming meditation gardens for the public to enjoy.

F. C. BEAMAN: A MAN OF VISION. F. C. Beaman was the man who placed the first park in Park City. It was Beaman who envisioned a vast park where the citizens of Knoxville could relax and enjoy the beautiful settings he created. His park offered a lake, caves to explore, mineral springs, a dance pavilion, and boating opportunities. What was once his private estate became Chilhowee Park. (Marge Beaman Jeffries.)

BEAMAN FAMILY CAMPERS. Clarence Beaman Sr. loved to take the family camping in the summer months to get away from the heat and humidity of the city. The land they used most often for these summer outings belonged to his father, F. C. Beaman, who held a considerable amount of land in and around Park City. (Marge Beaman Jeffries.)

COOLING OFF IN GRANDPA'S LAKE. Evelyn, Taylor, Libby, Dean, Alvin, Eloise, Jean, and their parents take a break from a hard day of camping to enjoy the cool water of Beaman Lake. What wonderful summer memories of ghost stories and campfires they described as they reminisced about the great times they had camping out at Beaman Lake. (Marge Beaman Jeffries.)

THE F. C. BEAMAN DAIRY FARM. This is how the Beaman dairy farm looked before the land was converted into a large pleasure park and lake. Beaman had already constructed the boathouse, seen across the lake, so that his friends and family could enjoy boating and picnicking on his land. One of the Beaman relatives lived in the log house pictured here and helped manage the farm. (Mabry Hazen Museum.)

A WORLD OF PROGRESS. The entrance to the 1910 Appalachian Exposition in Park City was the gateway to a well-planned event. Park City had become an incorporated municipality in 1907, and now, three years later, it was hosting a major national event. On opening day, 1,537 passengers arrived at the Southern Depot and 714 at the Louisville and Nashville (L&N) Depot to visit the exposition. (Charles M. Reeves.)

LONG VIEW OF LAKE OTTOSEE. This postcard illustrates the vast length of the original 14-acre spring-fed Lake Ottosee. In later years, the lake would be altered and diminished in size by local politicians. The park also had a number of caves and several mineral springs, which boasted of curative powers according to a brochure distributed in 1910. (Charles M. Reeves.)

NEGRO BUILDING. Knoxville College students constructed this impressive building for the Appalachian Exposition in 1910 at Chilhowee Park. The design and construction costs were paid for by the African American community. A parade led from Gay Street to Chilhowee Park where everyone celebrated the ribbon cutting for this imposing structure. This pavilion held exhibits that celebrated the culture and progress of black Americans at that time. (Charles M. Reeves.)

A POSTCARD FROM THE APPALACHIAN EXPOSITION. Families would have their photographs made during expositions and mail them back home to their loved ones. Since there were no hotels or motels available for the 10,000 African Americans who traveled here to attend the Exposition, many stayed in the homes of local families. (Beck Center.)

THE LIBERAL ARTS BUILDING. From 1910, when the first Appalachian Exposition was held at Chilhowee Park, until 1913, when the event was called the National Conservation Exposition, new buildings were added and others were enlarged to accommodate the growing importance of the park. The Liberal Arts Building had 84,000 square feet of exhibition space and overlooked the lake from the present site of the Jacob Building. (Charles M. Reeves.)

THE COAL BUILDING. Many of the buildings constructed for the three expositions highlighted specific industries, such as the Coal Building depicted, in this 1913 postcard image. Knoxville had a number of coal companies that pooled their resources to construct this building for the exposition. It was faced with large blocks of black coal, which glistened in the sunlight and became one of the most visited attractions at the exhibition. (Charles M. Reeves.)

CHILHOWEE PARK BANDSTAND. This beautiful marble bandstand was donated and constructed by the marble workers of Knoxville for the 1910 Appalachian Exposition at Chilhowee Park. By the 1940s, each of the elaborate exhibition halls was destroyed by fire. The bandstand is the only structure still in existence from the original expositions. It has been nicely restored and is still a lovely asset to the park. (Charles M. Reeves.)

BATHING BEACH AND LAKE. The bathing beach and lake were two of the most visited parts of Chilhowee Park in the years following the expositions. Park City residents would often ride the streetcar lines or walk to Chilhowee Park to swim in the summertime. Many young folks in Park City found summer employment at the park working as lifeguards or concessionaires to raise money for college tuition. (Charles M. Reeves.)

CELEBRATING THE APPALACHIAN EXPOSITION. Knoxville celebrated in grand style when the Appalachian Exposition came to Chilhowee Park in 1910. This horse-drawn wagon festooned with banners and ribbons parades past Charles McNabb's Marble City Motor Company, which was located at 319 West Main Street. (Beck Center.)

THE STABLES AT CHILHOWEE PARK. Fred Mynatt Sr. is shown driving a 10-pony hitch and wagon at Chilhowee Park. Mynatt operated a horse-riding stable there from the 1920s to the 1950s. He was featured in calendars and advertisements for Cas Walker and Service Cab Company and also showed horses for prominent Knoxvillians in various horse arenas. (Jerry Duncan/Gail Mynatt Ingram.)

RIDES AND ROLLER COASTER AT CHILHOWEE PARK. Amusements abounded at Chilhowee Park. The park offered a Ferris wheel, roller coaster, swings, a skating rink, a bowling alley, dodge 'em cars, penny arcades, and a beautiful merry-go-round with colorful horses. Boating was also a great way to spend the day, and Lake Ottosee was the perfect place. Young and old alike enjoyed a day at Chilhowee Park. (Jerry Duncan.)

INSIDE SMOKY'S BOWLING ALLEY. Joe "Smoky" Ellison (pictured), his wife, Bertha, and son, Joe, lived at 3435 Magnolia Avenue, as well as on Fifth Avenue, Washington Avenue, and in Burlington. Their son, Joe "Little Smoky" Ellison, later a major in the Air Force, was in East High's first graduating class in 1952, leaving Knoxville High as a senior. He described the final closing of Knoxville High as a heartbreaker. (Joe Ellison.)

SMOKY'S BOWLING ALLEY. Joe "Smoky" Ellison opened the first bowling alley in Knoxville in the 1930s at Chilhowee Park. Ellison was a concessionaire, operating batting games and other amusements in the park. Ollie and Effie May Bradley owned the Ferris wheel, fishpond, and dodge 'em games. Amusement rides and games were available to people in Park City every summer. (Joe Ellison.)

VAUGHN MONROE CROONS A TUNE. Well-known crooner Vaughn Monroe is shown here at Chilhowee Park. Best known for his fine rendition of *On Moonlight Bay*, he was extremely popular in the 1940s and 1950s and drew huge crowds. Many folks could be heard singing this song as they walked home along the sidewalks of Park City following his performances. Many concerts and events are still held at Chilhowee Park. (Jerry Duncan.)

DANCING UNDER THE STARS. Summertime dances were a frequent social activity at Chilhowee Park under this dance pavilion. Lovely tea dances and gala social gatherings were held here. Knoxville had many excellent bands that jumped at the opportunity to play at Chilhowee Park. (Charles M. Reeves.)

CHESTNUT VIEW PARK. This park, owned by Charles and Ethel Stafford, was a popular spot for the black community. The park was located on Chestnut Ridge, the site of present-day Adams Street, just north of Washington Avenue. The park is no longer there, but the magnificent view of Park City and the mountains beyond still exist. (Beck Center.)

CAL JOHNSON STOOD HERE. Caldonia "Cal" Fackler Johnson poses at the fountain at Cal Johnson Park in 1922. Born a slave at Colonel McClung's home on Gay Street in 1844, he worked the McClung horses in west Knox County. The skills he developed during his early years paid off later in life. According to the Beck Cultural Center, Johnson was one of the best "judges of horse flesh" in East Tennessee. (Beck Center.)

PARK CITY PONY RIDE. Two of the Beaman children go for a ride in their pony cart near Chilhowee Park. The pony was later given away in a contest sponsored by the Beaman Shoe Store located on Gay Street. The pony was never lacking in attention or tasty treats from the neighborhood children. (Marge Beaman Jeffries.)

53

A GRAND TOURING CAR. This grand touring car is parked on the grass at Speedway Circle in Burlington. Speedway Circle, owned by Cal Johnson the wealthiest African American in Tennessee, was once a horse racing track but was later used to race automobiles. Large crowds would gather there to enjoy the races and show off their own fancy cars. (Beck Center.)

EXPOSITION BOARDINGHOUSE. This scene depicts a boardinghouse in Park City during construction of the 1910 Appalachian Exposition. Many young men rode into town looking for work and liked Park City so well that they decided to stay and make this their home. They could see that Park City and Knoxville offered endless opportunity for ambitious, hard-working men and women. (Hoskins Library.)

Five

NEIGHBORHOODS

Park City, Mountain View, and Burlington are made up of many beautiful and diverse neighborhoods. These neighborhoods are distinguished not only by their architecture but by their ethnic and cultural interests as well.

By the 1890s, fashionable residential subdivisions were developed, including the East End Addition, Edgewood along Washington Avenue and Jefferson Avenue, and Elmwood Park between Edgewood and what was to become Magnolia Avenue.

East End, developed by the Strong and Thompson families, was described as "fourteen elegant residences" at the southeast corner of the state fairgrounds near Chestnut Street, with 50 by 150 foot lots on the fairgrounds itself. This was also the beginning of elegant homes being built on Magnolia Avenue in the Cold Spring Addition, a homage to the original Cold Springs Farm. Around the same time, F. C. Beaman and his partners were laying out plans for his residential subdivision, the Lake Park Springs addition, just west of Chilhowee Park along Woodbine, East Fifth, and Castle Streets.

The Elmwood Park Addition was south of the Edgewood development between Magnolia and Woodbine west of Bertrand. This neighborhood is not to be confused with Elmwood Avenue, just west of Chilhowee Park in the Chilhowee Park neighborhood.

Much has been said about the label "historic" and the way it seems to apply to so many different places. To some "historic" means ancient ruins, World War II battlefields, or even a historic school building like Park Junior High, now Park Place Condominiums. Sometimes it seems a difficult task to really define what "historic" means. Perhaps it is less important to ask, "Is this building historic?" and instead ask, "Is this building and is Park City worth saving?" Perhaps real preservation is nothing more than having the good sense to hang on to something, such as the Swans Bakery building on Magnolia or the charming Victorian homes (designed by George Barber) that can be found along Washington Avenue and Jefferson Avenue.

There other important homes on the other side of Magnolia as well, such as likely Barber-designed Victorians on Martin Luther King Jr. Boulevard or the charming 1930s apartment buildings on Magnolia Avenue. They are each important because they collectively define the historic character of the community. Most people buy a house or property because of what is around it, not just because of its own distinctive characteristics. Homeowners want green spaces and recreational spaces where they can enjoy walking, bicycle riding, or just leaning against a strong old shade tree and reading a good book. Park City offers many such parks and recreational areas throughout the community.

Park City, Mountain View, and Burlington offer abundant choices in neighborhoods and architecture, including Victorian, Craftsman-style bungalows, cottages, apartment complexes, duplexes, pre–Civil War homes, and condominiums. Many of these buildings are important simply because they are good to look at. As one author put it, they are "a gift to the street" whose style, textures, materials, and charm (and maybe even eccentricity) enrich and enliven their surroundings and the community. These properties are worth saving because our communities would be less interesting and less attractive without them.

Park City's buildings are worth saving because they have plenty of good use left in them. All across our city we can point out examples of what is known as "adaptive use" of long-neglected buildings. Old warehouses and retail buildings have been converted into apartments, restaurants, and trendy shops. Train stations have been converted into office space. Jewelry stores are converted into upscale bars and gathering places for downtown residents to unwind after a busy day at the office. This process has been good for the city and will be good for Park City also.

When the planners of Park City drew the first plans for the new subdivisions to be built, they took into consideration a number of things. They wanted beautifully landscaped parks and recreational areas and sidewalks for the children who used them while walking to school and the families who used them to stroll to church on Sunday morning. They wanted alleyways dividing the property lines at the backs of the homes, allowing a place to build a garage and provide the homeowner with safe off-street parking.

Today's modern subdivisions usually attach the garage to the end of the house facing the street. Such a street view offers the opportunity to see the entire contents of the garage when the door is left open. Things that can be seen might include a week's worth of garbage, kids' toys, and garden tools—not always a flattering view from the street. The planners of Park City took things like that into consideration and made sure that the homeowners were given alleys, sidewalks, street lights, and storm drains long before these things were even thought of in other areas of Knoxville. They created the perfect place in which to bring up a family. These factors helped Park City thrive and made its property extremely valuable for those who were fortunate enough to live there.

Park City offers a veritable feast for the true real-estate connoisseur. There are charming Victorian homes with all of the elegant mill work and ornate trim imaginable. There are spacious bungalows with inviting covered front porches, two-story four-square homes, Cape Cods, Dutch colonials, and stately brick and stone homes. There are also many duplexes and 1920s and 1930s apartment buildings. In Park City's glory days, these homes were immaculately kept inside and out. The yards were manicured and beautifully landscaped. Every kind of tree, shrub, and blooming flower could be found in Park City, and homeowners took great pride in the appearance of their property. These wonderful houses still stand in Park City, just waiting for someone to give them a chance to shelter another generation of homeowners.

THE BEAMAN HOME. This beautiful home was designed by George Barber and built especially for the Beaman family in 1910 at 3041 Magnolia Avenue. Clarence Beaman Sr. owned Beaman's Shoe Store on Gay Street. He and his wife, Cora, had six children and always graciously welcomed people for Sunday dinner. Even during the Depression, the Beaman home was alive with family and friends who sought refuge from the lean years by renting rooms from the Beamans. (Marge Beaman Jeffries.)

BECK HOMES IN MOUNTAIN VIEW. James and Ethel Beck owned a number of fine homes in Mountain View along Mabry Hill including this home, believed to be on Patton Street just north of Mabry Hill. (Beck Center.)

A MOUNTAIN VIEW HOME. This home in Mountain View was also owned by James and Ethel Beck. It was razed in the 1980s during urban renewal, which many now regard as "urban destruction." (Beck Center.)

BECK HOME ON SUMMIT HILL. James and Ethel Beck were two of the most glamorous and influential members of Knoxville's black community of the 1920s, 1930s, and 1940s. The Becks were in the forefront of black civic, church, and social activities. The Becks were involved in the establishment of the Knoxville Colored Orphanage in 1919, later known as Ethel Beck Home for Children. They acquired vast real-estate holdings in the east Knoxville area. (Beck Center.)

BLACKBERRY CORNER. Margery and Mike Bensey currently own the home at 1702 East Fifth Avenue in the Elmwood Park Addition of Park City. When they bought it about 15 years ago, they named it Blackberry Corner in honor of the lush gardens on the property and the Black family, who built the home in 1910. (Margery Bensey.)

STERCHI-HUMPHREY HOUSE IN BIDDLE HEIGHTS. Built by the Sterchi family, Stephen and Grace Humphrey purchased this large bungalow at 500 Biddle Street in the Biddle Heights development. Alice Ruth Warrell, a well-known historian and preservationist in Sweetwater, grew up in this fine home backing up to Howell Nurseries, which the family would often use for picnics. (Stephen Humphrey Jr./Alice R. Worrell.)

ASTON APARTMENTS. This 1941 photograph shows the exterior of the Aston Apartments at 2736 Magnolia Avenue. Arthur Fernando Aston was born in 1891, the son of Jacob Aston and Ruth Beaman. In 1924, Aston lived at 3127 McCalla Avenue, while Herbert Aston lived at 2806 Linden Avenue. They were partners in the Aston Jobbing Company and also the Aston Candy Company. Aston also built the Lakewood Apartments at 2730 Magnolia in 1929 and the Shenandoah Apartments at 2724 Magnolia in 1930. Aston was the father of Barbara Aston-Wash, well-known society columnist for the *Knoxville News Sentinel*. The Aston Apartments are now owned by Bittle and Sons Construction, who plan to convert the building into condominiums. Notable Knoxvillians such as Mary Costa started life in these fashionable apartments. (McClung Collection.)

LOOKING EAST ON MAGNOLIA AVENUE. This photograph was taken March 3, 1939, and is an excellent example of the mixture of business and residential on Magnolia Avenue at that time. Notice the streetcar crossing Magnolia. (McClung Collection.)

THE W. J. SAVAGE HOME. Ina Fern Fields Wayland Savage bought this small house at 2812 Woodbine Avenue with her new husband, W. J. Savage, after their wedding. Mr. Savage had been living in a downtown hotel before their marriage. They wanted a small house of their own. Mr. Savage is in the picture with their granddaughter, Anne Wayland, who was about 12 at the time. (Anne Wayland Lambert.)

HOMES ON DANDRIDGE AVENUE IN MOUNTAIN VIEW. These stately homes were located in the town of Mountain View on Dandridge Avenue across from the Mabry Hazen house. They were razed in the 1980s to make way for the construction of Morningside Park and the placement of the Alex Haley statue. The Park City and Morningside areas need to be made priorities for historic preservation. Large homes similar to these abound throughout the area and many are presently being restored to their original beauty. (Mabry Hazen Museum.)

A HOME IN MOUNTAIN VIEW. This home may have been located on Rosedale Street near the Mabry Hazen House. Before being known as the Morningside community, the area from First Creek out Dandridge Pike along Mabry Hill was known as the town of Mountain View. (Mabry Hazen Museum.)

ON MAGNOLIA. Stanley Levy, a civil engineer for the Southern Railroad, arrives at 2922 Magnolia. E. O. Guthrie, who owned several Appalachian coal mines, lived across the street. Ben Harrison lived nearby. His family would later own Harrison's Chicken City. Kenneth Needham's wife, Christine, another neighbor, baked cakes at Woolworth's on Gay Street and later started a catering business. (Richard M. Licht.)

JOHN BRICHETTO AND DAUGHTER. Lawrence Brichetto's brother, John, arrives with his daughter at Lawrence's home at 3201 East Fifth Avenue. The home shown in the background was so lavishly decorated each Christmas that traffic would be backed up for blocks as folks drove by to see the festive displays. (David Brichetto.)

THE WAYLAND HOME. This is another view of the Woodward/Wayland home at 511 North Castle Street in Park City. The Waylands had six sons and one daughter and needed all the room they could get. The roof of the home was constructed of terra-cotta tiles, which were a quite expensive feature. During the Civil War, soldiers camped out on this property and also in the adjacent area, which would become Chilhowee Park. (Anne Wayland Lambert.)

FIFTH AND CASTLE. This fine bungalow was built by Clarence Beaman Sr. in the Lake Park Springs Addition at the corner of East Fifth Avenue and Castle Street, on the eastern edge of Park City. (Marge Beaman Jeffries/Thompson Photo.)

Winter 1941. Pictured here is the home of John Woodward Pickell and Helen Huffine, located at 3019 (now 3037) East Fifth Avenue in Park City. This photograph was taken in 1941, following a winter snowstorm. (Helen Pickell Lobertini Schaich.)

PARK CITY   NO. 6.   EAST KNOXVILLE NO. 4.

East Knoxville and Park City Fire Departments. Fire Station No. 4 was located on Reservoir Hill on Clinch Avenue, near the present-day Regency Apartments. The fire engine is a 1934 open cab, which has been restored and is used in modern parades by the Knoxville Fire Department. Park City's fire station was located on Linden Avenue just to the left of Park Lowry Grammar School, and it became known as Fire Station No. 6 after annexation in 1917. (Jerry Duncan.)

THE DUNCAN FAMILY HOME. Mildred Phillips Frances Duncan's home, located at 2014 Linden Avenue, is pictured here. It was at his grandmother's house that Jerry Duncan spent many an afternoon playing along Linden Avenue. (Jerry Duncan.)

BILLY MEYER STADIUM. Bill Meyer Stadium, or "Billy Meyer" to its fans, was built in 1955, the year that the old Caswell Park stands burned. A classic example of minor league ballpark architecture, it seated over 6,000 fans. Standard Knitting Mills loomed over the left field wall, its windows a target for right-handed power hitters. William Adam Meyer was born in Knoxville, Tennessee, on January 14, 1892. A catcher, Meyer began his professional career with the hometown Knoxville Reds in 1910. Bill Meyer played for the White Sox and A's in 1916 and 1917, and managed minor-league teams until 1947, when he was picked to manage the Pittsburgh Pirates. A month after Meyer's death in 1957, the city of Knoxville renamed the ballpark "Bill Meyer Stadium." (Jerry Duncan.)

LINDEN AVENUE STREETSCAPE. This 1950s photograph shows the lovely homes of Linden Avenue. Notable families like the Regas, Psihogios, Corkrans, Sharps, the Tom Blacks, and Judge Kelly and his wife, Janie, lived on Linden. It is one street south of Magnolia Avenue and was considered extremely desirable in terms of its real estate and close proximity to Park City Lowry Grammar School. (Thompson Photo.)

MAGNOLIA AVENUE 1953. This lovely streetscape shows the types of homes that could be seen on Magnolia Avenue in the 1950s. As the years passed, Magnolia became a combination of homes and businesses, which provided the perfect mix for the neighborhood. As a strong business corridor in 2005, there are still quite a few large homes on Magnolia suitable for professional offices, such as law or accounting practices. (Thompson Photo.)

THE LOBETTI HOME ON EAST FIFTH AVENUE. Joseph and Minnie Lobetti and their 10 children lived in this stately seven-bedroom home that still stands at 2701 East Fifth Avenue. This photograph was taken in the winter of 1937. Mr. Lobetti had arrived in Knoxville as an Italian immigrant and decided to make Park City his home. This property is an excellent example of the type of real estate that is abundant throughout the area. (Robert Mose Lobetti.)

THE ASTON HOME ON MAGNOLIA AVENUE. Arthur Fernando Aston and his wife, Clara Nelle (Burnette), lived in this fine home at 1520 Magnolia Avenue. They first lived in the Aston Apartments, which he built with his brothers Herbert and Fred. Aston continued to build homes in Park City, Holston Hills, and Sequoyah Hills until the stock market crash of 1929. He then went to work for the Tennessee Valley Authority and the Oak Ridge complex. (Barbara Aston-Wash.)

Six

SCHOOLS AND CHURCHES

The schools and churches of Park City, Mountain View, and Burlington have always played a vital role in the lives and futures of the residents of these neighborhoods. Most of these schools and churches were built from 1900 to 1940. Many of them are still in existence and still stand in their original locations. Sadly some have been lost to urban renewal and development. This chapter represents a collection of both the schools and churches that still exist as well as a sampling of those that have been lost during the past several years.

Park City, Mountain View, and Burlington were designed as "walking neighborhoods" from their beginnings in the late 19th century. People established neighborhoods conducive to foot traffic because very few folks had any form of transportation other that walking. Even in later years (1920s), when automobiles became commonplace, most people still walked. The schools and churches were placed in the center of neighborhoods because those were the places where most community activity took place. Fund-raisers were common when new band uniforms were needed or some other expense needed to be met.

The churches were the social backbone of the community. The local churches sponsored picnics, hayrides, and Wednesday-night prayer-meeting suppers for their membership. The churches were also the place where beautiful and elaborate weddings and baby christenings were held. In the era prior to funeral homes, it was not uncommon for someone's funeral to be held at the neighborhood church.

Many of the people interviewed while writing this book seem to have fond memories of the chiming church bells that could be heard throughout Park City on Sunday mornings. The bells also rang out loud and long when World Wars I and II ended, and they tolled along with churches citywide when Franklin Roosevelt died suddenly in Warm Springs, Georgia, in 1945. The sounds of wonderful choirs and gospel music filling the air during revivals seem permanently embedded in the hearts and memories of most Park Citians.

PLAY BALL. Baseball was a popular sport in Knoxville. This photograph shows the boys from Burlington Baptist Church proudly sporting the infamous double-B on the front of their shirts. Most community teams played ball at Caswell Park or Chilhowee Park. Local factories and merchants would sponsor baseball teams, and the whole community would come out to watch them play. (Ernie, Bob, and Debbie Barnes.)

AUSTIN HIGH SCHOOL. Emily Austin established Austin High School in 1879 at 327 Central Street to educate young blacks. In 1916, the Knoxville Colored High School was built on Payne Avenue. In 1928, a new Austin High School was built on Vine Street. The building pictured was constructed in 1951 and is now the Vine Middle Magnet School. During desegregation in 1968, the board of education combined Austin High with all-white East High. The school was renamed Austin East High School. (Beck Center.)

ST. CLAIR COBB AND THE AUSTIN HIGH BAND. Austin High School had a notable band for many years. St. Clair Cobb was the band director who taught many musicians in the area. He also started the Elks Band. Cobb was serious about his craft, and it was not uncommon for a student who hit a wrong note to get popped on the head with a drumstick. (Beck Center.)

CHARLES WARNER CANSLER. Born in Maryville, Tennessee, in 1871, Cansler's mother, Laura Scott Cansler, was Knoxville's first black school teacher in 1864, when she got permission from Union general Ambrose Burnside to open a school for free blacks. Charles began teaching at Austin High School in 1900 and became principal in 1912. The same year, he organized the East Tennessee Association of Teachers in Colored Schools. He was the leader in getting the Andrew Carnegie Foundation to establish a library for blacks in 1917. In 1919, he influenced the state legislature to pass an act enabling descendants of ex-slaves to inherit real estate. Known as a mathematical wizard, Charles traveled the country to give demonstrations of his skills in beating an adding machine by mentally adding tall numeric columns. (Beck Center.)

JAZZ SINGER ETTA MOTEN BARNETT. Etta Moten Barnett visits Austin High School in the 1940s. She went on to achieve stardom in the theater, performing in many legendary Broadway productions. Moten became the first African American stage and screen star to sing and perform at the White House, when President and Mrs. Franklin D. Roosevelt invited her on January 31, 1933. (Beck Center.)

CARNEGIE LIBRARY. The Carnegie Library was built in 1917 on Vine Avenue with funds from the Andrew Carnegie Foundation. It was built under the leadership of Charles Warner Cansler, principal of Austin High School. "Colored" Carnegie libraries represented a step forward for the black community but illustrated the tension between academic advancement and segregation. Other cities building Carnegie Libraries included Louisville, Houston, Nashville, and New York City's Harlem. (Beck Center.)

DISTINGUISHED GENTLEMEN. In this 1914 photograph, W. E. B. DuBois, a founder of the NAACP, visited Knoxville. Pictured from left to right are Charles Warner Cansler, DuBois, William Yardley, W. M. Brooks, Rev. Black, Howard Carter, Mr. Graves, Dr. S. M. Clark, Dr. J. H. Presnell, Rev. J. Byers, and one unidentified person. (Beck Center.)

EASTPORT SCHOOL, 1910. This 1910 photograph depicts a class in front of the original Eastport School, a black public school established in 1905 on Fuller Street in the Eastport community of Park City. The school graduated its first high school class in 1916 and, by some accounts, was called Eastport High School. The fine brick Eastport school building on Bethel Avenue replaced the original structure in 1932. (Beck Center.)

GREEN SCHOOL. Green Elementary was built in 1909 to alleviate crowding at the original Austin School on Central Street. It became the Knoxville Colored High School in 1916. In 1928, it became a junior high school with grades three through eight and had an adult night school. When Vine Junior High School opened in 1952, it returned to being an elementary school. In 1993, the school became a magnet school. (Beck Center.)

LOGAN TEMPLE AME ZION CHURCH. This church was located on Reservoir Hill prior to urban renewal. Logan Temple AME Zion is now at 2744 Selma Avenue and is a major force for change along with Greater Warner Tabernacle AME Zion. Together the two churches operate the AME Zion Church Center on Magnolia Avenue, which includes a full-service bookstore, credit union, travel agency, print shop, and professional offices. (Beck Center.)

MOUNT ZION BAPTIST CHURCH ON PATTON STREET. Mount Zion Baptist Church was established in 1860. It is one of Knoxville's oldest black Baptist churches. Poet Nikki Giovanni's poem, "Don't Worry, There's No Racial Hatred Here" recounts her memories of the church. Its founders once attended First Baptist Church, when during the Civil War, black members formed their own church. The church relocated from Patton Street to Brooks Road in 1967. (Beck Center.)

FIRST BLACK PRESBYTERIAN CHURCH IN THE SOUTH. Established in 1865 on the corner of Henley and Clinch, Shiloh Presbyterian first met on the back porch of Perez Dickinson's mansion. It moved to Reservoir Hill on Church Street in 1930. Following urban renewal, it is now located at 904 Biddle Street. A charter member, James Mason, a freed slave in Knox County, was saving money to buy his wife's freedom when slavery was abolished. He used the money to buy a house, becoming Knoxville's first black taxpayer in 1866. (Beck Center.)

TABERNACLE BAPTIST CHURCH. Tabernacle Baptist Church was established in 1912. It moved to the corner of Florida and Campbell Streets, then to a tent at 600 Campbell Street. In 1915, 83 congregants were baptized in one day. The congregation hired three streetcars to Hill Avenue, where they marched to the Tennessee River for baptizing. In 1951, the church was rebuilt at the corner of Vine and Keller Street. (Beck Center.)

PARK CITY BAPTIST CHURCH. Park City Baptist Church was organized in 1927 at 2519 Selma Avenue, illustrating the importance of the Park City name even after annexation in 1917. Rev. Louis O. Ball was its pastor. In 1941, there were nearly 60 churches in the Park City, Mountain View, and Burlington areas. (Jerry Duncan.)

A Graduating Class at Park City High School. Pictured is a group of graduating seniors standing in front of Park City High School *c.* 1909. It became a grammar school after Knoxville High School was built on Fifth Avenue in 1910. (Anne Wayland Lambert.)

Park City High School. Pictured here is one of the graduating classes of Park City High School. This photograph shows the front steps of the school, and based on the clothing of those shown, this photograph was probably taken sometime in the first decade of the 20th century. (Hoskins Library.)

PARK CITY HIGH SCHOOL. This handsome, imposing structure was built in 1907, and for a brief time, it was as Knoxville's largest high school. Ina Fields Wayland, Park City historian, reported that the school was one of the largest public schools in the South, with an enrollment of 1,700 white students and 500 African American students. After becoming Park Lowry Grammar School, where many Knoxville children attended, the school board decided to close this school in 1982 and transfer the students to the more modern Sara Moore Greene School. The building was sold at auction to private contractors in the mid 1980s, but their plans never reached full development. In September 1987, Park City Lowry School caught fire, and although the main building was unharmed, it was later razed. It seems an ignoble end for such a important part of Park City's history. Of all the buildings lost to Park City over the years, this magnificent structure is perhaps the greatest loss of all. (Lillian Mashburn.)

SCHOOL DAYS AT PARK LOWRY GRAMMAR. Childhood friends Richard Licht (left) and Bill Zwick (right) emerge from school at Park Lowry Grammar. The Zwicks lived in the 3000 block of Magnolia Avenue on the north side. Bill had two older sisters, Carol and Barbara, and their father, Ben Zwick, ran a produce company on Forest Avenue called House of Abe. The Zwicks were the first family Richard knew that had an outdoor swimming pool. (Richard M. Licht.)

FOUNTAIN INSTALLATION AT PARK CITY SCHOOL. During the days of dreaded polio epidemics, the lunchroom at Park City Lowry Grammar School on Linden Avenue was as germ-free as it got. As seen in this 1941 photograph, a lunchroom worker would squirt liquid soap, and the children would then circle the fountain scrubbing and rinsing their hands. The ritual was completed when each child was handed a paper towel by his teacher. (McClung Collection.)

PARK CITY GIRLS BASKETBALL. The 1911 Park City High girls basketball team, as they appeared in *Kalendar*, the school yearbook, is shown here. Note the PCHS logo on their sweaters. Imagine playing basketball in sweaters and skirts with hair bows in your hair. (Lillian Mashburn.)

FIFTH AVENUE BAPTIST CHURCH. Fifth Avenue Baptist Church, located at the corner of Chestnut Street and East Fifth Avenue, is a thriving neighborhood church with a large and loyal congregation. This beautiful church still plays a vital role in the neighborhood and now offers a day care center for working parents in the area. (Jerry Duncan.)

MAGNOLIA METHODIST CHURCH. This magnificent Gothic style church is located at the corner of Magnolia Avenue and Harrison Street. Beautiful organ music and stirring chimes are heard each Sunday morning in Park City from this church just east of Cherry Street. Many of its parishioners lived in the neighborhood and found it most convenient to walk to church on Sunday mornings. (Jerry Duncan.)

PARK JUNIOR HIGH SCHOOL. Park Junior High School is located on Bertrand Street in Park City. In the late 1980s, a public auction was held. Christopher Kendrick purchased the building and began the process of converting it into charming condominiums. It is now known as Park Place, a lovely gated condominium complex. Kendrick's vision for this property illustrates both the historical and financial arguments for revitalizing Park City. (Jerry Duncan.)

KNOXVILLE HIGH SCHOOL. Designed by Baumann and Baumann in 1910, some of Knoxville's most prominent citizens graduated from Knoxville High School (KHS). This building at the corner of Central Avenue and East Fifth Avenue is now home to the Knoxville Board of Education. Evans-Collins Field, adjacent to Caswell Park, was named in honor of KHS principal W. E. Evans and KHS head football coach Wilson Collins. (Hoskins Library.)

PRINCIPAL OF KNOXVILLE HIGH SCHOOL. W. E. Evans and his wife, Helen, are shown in front of their home at 3036 Magnolia Ave. W. E. Evans was principal of Knoxville High School from 1914 until it closed its doors as a school in the early 1960s. The Evans family lived on Magnolia Avenue, and all four of the Evans children attended KHS. (John Evans.)

Seven

THE FAMILY BUSINESS

Entrepreneurship and self-reliance were the lifeblood that built not only Park City but also much of Knoxville. From its birth, many of Knoxville's influential business leaders, politicians, doctors, and attorneys hailed from Park City. Even after the annexation of Park City in 1917, the number of businesses in Park City that include "Park City" in their name continued to increase.

Frank and Edith Regas lived at 2058 East Fifth Avenue until the late 1920s and moved to 2643 Linden Avenue around 1945. Frank's brother, George, and his wife, Penny, lived next door. The next generation, Bill, Gus, and Harry Regas, grew up on Linden. The Regases started a small coffee shop downtown in 1919 that still operates today as Regas Restaurant, one of the finest landmark restaurants in the region. Dave Thomas, the late founder of the Wendy's restaurant chain, worked there when he was 13.

Many of the fine homes of the community are still standing along such streets as Woodbine Avenue and East Fifth Avenue. The charming brick and stone home at 515 Beaman Street that once belonged to Abe and Helen Schwartz is an excellent example of the types of homes that are plentiful throughout Park City, and it further illustrates the relationship between residents of Park City and their family businesses in downtown Knoxville. The glass elevator, that rises up the side of the home was installed in later years, after Mr. Schwartz had a stroke. He was the owner of the Vogue Department Store in downtown Knoxville.

The families of Park City, Mountain View, and Burlington have been the founders of some of the oldest, most prominent businesses in Knoxville. They knew the fine art of networking even before that phrase had been coined, and they attributed much of their success to their ability to network with fellow neighbors who were bankers, landowners, wholesalers, and possible future customers of their fledgling enterprises.

BOYD BROWDER. Boyd Browder was Knoxville's most important black photographer. Browder excelled at portrait photography and photographs of human interest, especially within the black community. He was a contemporary of Jim Thompson, one of Knoxville's first commercial photographers. Browder was elected to the Knox County Court from 1942 to 1946. (Beck Center.)

LUNCH AT THE ATLANTA CAFÉ. Park City residents Nick Passiakos and James Psihogios (pronounced *sa-hoy-yus*) opened the Atlanta Café in downtown Knoxville in the 1920s. At one time, most restaurants in Knoxville were operated by the Greek community, who were attracted by the mountains that reminded them of Greece. The Atlanta Café was sold to another Greek family in 1972, it but closed in the late 1970s. (Pete Psihogios.)

CARTOON WEDDING CAR. Cartoonist and Park City resident David Broome Huffine illustrated this car for his sister, Helen, on the day she married John Woodward Pickell in 1927. The car is in the driveway of the Huffine-Pickell home on East Fifth Avenue. Huffine worked for the *Saturday Evening Post*, *American Magazine*, *Liberty*, and *Collier's*. (Helen Pickell Lobertini Schaich.)

CAL JOHNSON BUILDING. The Cal Johnson Building was located at the corner of Vine and Central Avenues. The building was home to at least three attorneys, seven doctors, and two dentists, as well as being the location of the Universal Life Insurance Company, the New York Café, and a drugstore. In the foreground, a 1920s traffic control tower is visible. (Beck Center.)

BEFORE URBAN RENEWAL. Prior to urban renewal in the 1960s, the Bowery district now known as the Old City was a vibrant black business community with hardware stores, barbershops, pharmacies, and professional offices for doctors and attorneys. Patrick Sullivan's Saloon, at the corner of Central and Jackson, is visible in the far left of this 1950s photograph of Central Avenue. (Beck Center.)

DOGAN-GAITHER MOTEL. The Dogan-Gaither Motel was another black-owned motel, depicted in this 1954 photograph when it was located on Vine Avenue. It later moved to a newer building on Jessamine Street. (Beck Center.)

THE GEM THEATRE. The original Gem Theatre opened in 1913 as a silent movie house at 102 Vine Avenue. The Gem Theatre in this photograph opened in 1921. It was the oldest black theatre in Knoxville, and stars such as Billie Holiday, Bessie Smith, Ethel Waters, Cab Calloway, Dinah Washington, Dewey Pigmeat (*Here Come De Judge*) Markham, Mantan Moreland, F. E. Miller, and local Fred Logan entertained audiences with live shows. The original Gem, which burned in 1939, seated over 2,000 people. It featured an orchestra pit and an large stage. The only other theatres in Knoxville with such features were the Tennessee and the Bijou. The Gem was rebuilt in 1940 with a smaller stage, no orchestra pit, and a much smaller seating capacity. (Beck Center.)

GLEANER PRINTING COMPANY ON EAST VINE. The Gleaner Printing Company was a black-owned business located on East Vine Avenue east of the present-day Old City. (Beck Center.)

INSIDE EASLEY'S GROCERY. This *c.* 1930 photograph shows the inside of Alfred and Eva Easley's grocery store at 1112 East Vine Avenue. They lived at 409 Lithgoe, which was near Payne Avenue, where Austin Homes is today. Many homeowners and black-owned businesses like this one did not survive urban renewal. (Beck Center.)

JARNIGAN AND SON. As early as 1876, Clement Jarnigan was learning the undertaking business at L. C. Shephard Undertakers. He started his own funeral business on Nelson Street in 1886. Today Jarnigan and Son is one of the oldest continuously operating black-owned businesses in Knoxville, operating at 2823 Martin Luther King Jr. Avenue. (Beck Center.)

LINDSAY'S CONFECTIONERY. Lindsay's Confectionery was located on McCalla Avenue across from the old Austin High School. They offered the best hot dogs in the world and fried baloney sandwiches with onion. Soft drinks on ice were so cold they would freeze your hand off trying to get one. Notice Austin Homes in the background of the photo. (Beck Center.)

MEDICAL ARTS BUILDING. The Medical Arts Building on Vine Avenue was the black community's equivalent to the other one located on Main Street. Here African American doctors, dentists, and attorneys practiced their trades. In 1948, tenants included Dr. E. F. Lennon; S. A. Curren, DDS; Dr. J. H. Clark; J. A. Huff, attorney; C. A. Cowan, attorney; Dr. A. J. Bacote; Dr. O. B. Taylor; and G. W. McDade, attorney. Adjacent to this professional building was the New York Café, the Gem Barber Shop, and the Gem Beauty Shop. (Beck Center.)

GRABBING A SANDWICH AT THE PRESNELL BUILDING. A typical lunchtime at the sandwich shop located in the Presnell Building is pictured here. (Beck Center.)

SYLVESTER MCBEE'S FRUIT STAND. Sylvester McBee proudly strikes a pose in front of his fruit stand at 701 East Vine Avenue. McBee began as a porter for the Rebori family on Clinch Avenue, but, by 1923, he was a deputy sheriff boarding at 927 East Vine. He opened his grocery in 1925. Even in this black-and-white photograph, the produce just glistens. (Beck Center.)

VINE AVENUE SERVICE STATION. This service station was located on Vine Avenue in this 1929 photograph. By the early 20th century, blacks in Knoxville were operating many successful businesses, including taxi companies, building contractors, street contractors, printers, newspapers, auto repair shops, shoe shops, funeral parlors, barber shops, beauty shops, restaurants, grocery stores, a soft drink bottling company, dry cleaners, boarding houses, pool rooms, and taverns. (Beck Center.)

WJBE AND THE GODFATHER OF SOUL. WJBE Radio at 2402 McCalla Avenue was one of three radio stations owned by soul singer James Brown. Brown purchased the station in 1968 and brought Jimmy Clark from Augusta, Georgia, to run it as disc jockey Clark Jaye. Clark said WJBE and the Five Points area of Park City boosted each other. Clark would later open Jimmy Who's Music Maker record store and several nightclubs in Five Points and Burlington. (Beck Center.)

INSIDE STANDARD KNITTING MILLS, 1945. Standard Knitting Mills was once one of the largest employers in all of Park City. Established in 1900 by E. E. McMillan on Washington Avenue, the mill ran three shifts seven days per week during the war years to keep up with the demand for their product. At its peak, it occupied over 600,000 square feet and employed over 3,000 workers. It remained in operation until 1989. In addition to men's underwear, it manufactured sleepwear, sportswear, and fleece shirts. (McClung Collection.)

STANDARD KNITTING MILLS. This photograph of Standard Knitting Mills was made in December 1952 and shows the exterior of this fine building. There was a small public outcry when the mill was razed, but it was not strong enough to save this fine building. (McClung Collection.)

1944 PRESIDENTIAL CAMPAIGN. In 1944, the Dr. James H. Presnell Medical Building at 503 East Vine Avenue served as the local Democratic Party headquarters. Presnell, Knoxville's "Bronze Mayor" as he was called, was very popular during the 1930s and 1940s. A 1910 Knoxville College graduate, he fought efforts to destroy beautiful homes and prosperous businesses during Knoxville's urban renewal projects. Presnell also worked to reduce school overcrowding and address the perpetual flooding of First Creek. (Beck Center.)

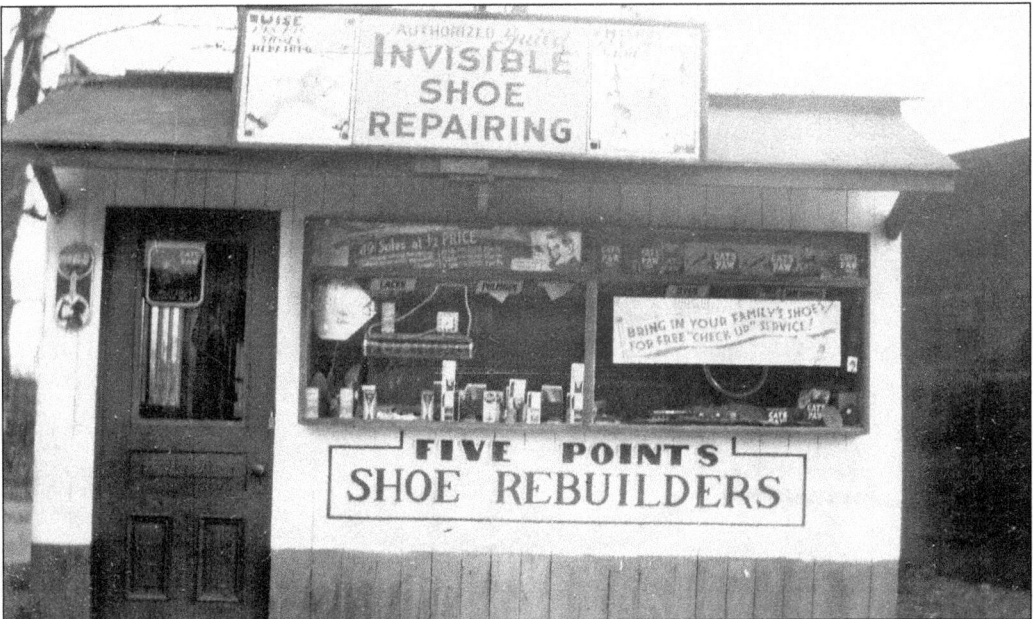

FIVE POINTS SHOE SHOP. This shoe shop in Five Points is an example of many of the strong family businesses located throughout Park City and east Knoxville early in the 20th century. (Jerry Duncan/David Oxendine.)

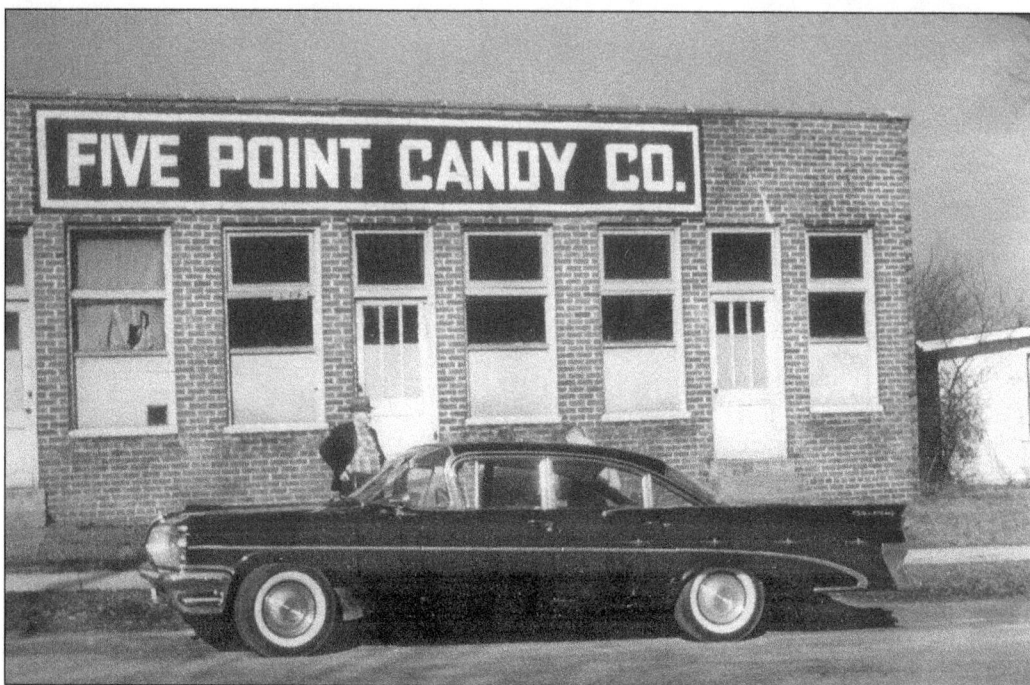

FIVE POINTS CANDY COMPANY. Five Points Candy Company was located in the busy business section of Five Points and manufactured a variety of candies. There have been many prosperous manufacturing businesses located in the Five Points area since the early 1920s. (Jerry Duncan.)

HAPPY DAYS IN PARK CITY. You can almost hear "Rock Around the Clock" in this 1950s photograph at the Gulf Service Station located at the corner of Magnolia Avenue and Kyle Street. Gasoline was about 18¢ per gallon in those days, and folks did not worry about big cars with powerful engines in this age of family automobiles and long trips across the country. (Jerry Duncan.)

REGAS RESTAURANT. The Regas family lived for many years on Linden Avenue in Park City, establishing their restaurant in the Watauga Hotel at the corner of Gay and Magnolia. It was conveniently located across the street from the once-thriving Southern Depot, where passenger trains brought visitors to and from Knoxville. Around 1956, the upper floors of the hotel were removed. As a counterman, Bill Regas remembers competing for tips with a teenaged Dave Thomas, founder of the Wendy's restaurant chain. The adjacent five-story Hotel Atkin was razed to make room for a 177-space parking lot, which has allowed the Regas to stay downtown for the last 86 years. (Bill Regas.)

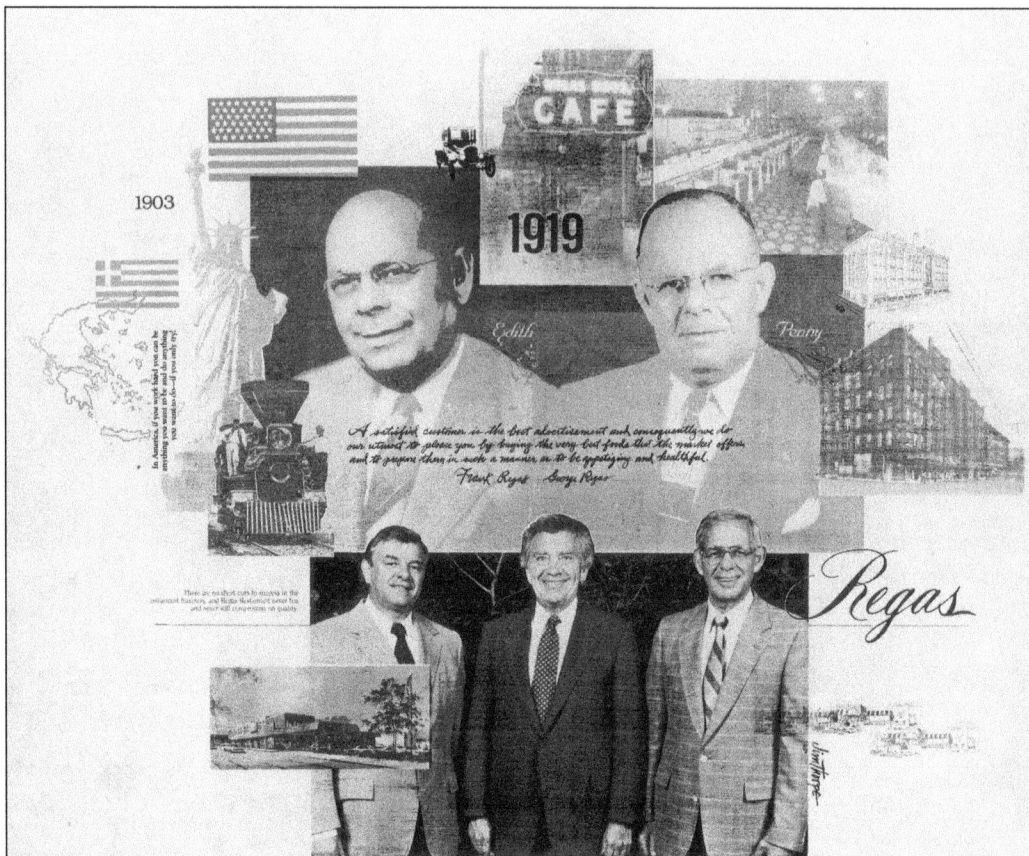

THREE GENERATIONS. Frank, George, and Harry Regas came to America from Greece in 1903 and started the Astor Café inside the Hotel Watauga at the corner of Gay and Magnolia in 1919. It was later known as Regas Brothers Café and was renamed Regas Restaurant in 1938. In the 1950s, Bill Regas, son of Frank, started working there and, by 1980, was president of the National Restaurant Association. Bill's son Grady would start a national chain of Grady's restaurants. (Bill Regas.)

NASH DRY CLEANERS. Nash Dry Cleaners was located on McCalla Avenue, now Martin Luther King Jr. Boulevard, in Park City. The building still stands at the west end of Austin East High School; however, it now belongs to Jacob "Budd" Watson and is now called Ideal Cleaners. From the 1950s, the Nash family always cleaned the East High band uniforms at a reduced rate and were considered boosters for the high school. (Jerry Duncan.)

USHERS AT THE PARK THEATRE. Jerry Duncan (right) and a friend worked as ushers at the Park Theater, located at the corner of Olive Street and Magnolia Avenue. This little neighborhood theater was the center of activity on Saturday mornings, when it hosted the "Kiddie Club" for community children. On Saturdays, the children were treated to double features of westerns, horror movies, and comedy films. (Jerry Duncan.)

PIZZA PALACE. Charlie Peroulas (left), his father Arthur (middle), and uncle Al (right) are hard at work at the Pizza Palace at 3132 East Magnolia Avenue in Park City. Brothers Arthur, Al, and Gus Peroulas came to Park City from Greece in the mid-1950s, opening Pizza Palace in 1961. The three brothers and their families lived together on Linden Avenue at the corner of Harrison Street. (Charlie Peroulas.)

PARK CITY'S FIRST ITALIAN RESTAURANT. For many in Park City and Knoxville, Pizza Palace was their first experience with a pizza. The brothers opened Pero's Steak House on Kingston Pike in 1963. It closed in 1994. Arthur passed away in 2002 and Al in 2003. Gus is retired and lives in west Knoxville. The family continues to operate the business today, which is one of the oldest restaurants still operating on Magnolia Avenue. (Charlie Peroulas.)

ASTON PAINT STORE. Resourceful entrepreneurs like Arthur Fernando Aston operated multiple businesses, especially after the Depression. Here Aston attends his paint store, which he developed in the carriage house behind the Aston home at 1520 Magnolia Avenue. (Barbara Aston-Wash.)

TIC TOC DRIVE-IN. The Tic Toc Restaurant and Drive-In was one of the most popular places in Park City. It was a family business owned by Ernie, Bob, and Betty Carr. Such notables as Archie Campbell, Lowell Blanchard, Hank Williams Sr., Kenny Rogers, and Gov. George Wallace enjoyed the excellent cuisine offered at the Tic Toc. Sadly it has now closed. (Betty Carr.)

WALKER'S BAR-B-Q. Julius Walker (left) and his son, Hugh, are pictured here in 1928 in front of Walker's Bar-B-Q at 3225 Magnolia Avenue. Born in 1873, Julius Walker operated a saloon in Rome, Georgia, before moving to Park City. The Walkers sold beer, soft drinks, and barbecue on "butter toasted sandwiches" at this location from 1914 until after Julius's death in 1955. (Charlie and Sue Walker.)

INSIDE BARNES BARBER SHOP. Every chair is occupied in this May 6, 1930, photograph inside Barnes Barber Shop. The barbers working this day are R.C. Barnes, Joe Cross, M.B. Robinson, and Cas Walker. The shoeshine stand is operated by Charlie Debro. The business is located at 3918 McCalla Avenue where it has existed for 79 years under the Barnes family ownership. It is the oldest business in existence in Burlington. (Ernie, Bob, and Debbie Barnes.)

FROM TIN CANS TO TELEVISION. Clarence Beaman Jr. (top), brother Alvin (middle), and an unidentified friend pose at the Beaman home on Magnolia Avenue. Always interested in communications, Beaman once rigged up tin cans and some wires in the neighborhood. He was owner of WKGN Radio from 1947 to 1955 and founded WATE TV 6, Knoxville's first television station, in 1953. Beaman later owned Clarence Beaman Realty. (Marge Beaman Jeffries.)

WHEELER FUNERAL HOME. A. R. Wheeler and Son Funeral Home was a prominent mortuary in the heart of Knoxville's black residential and commercial district. (Beck Center.)

PONY CARTS IN PARK CITY. Kay's Ice Cream Company's full fleet of pony carts is ready for business. The company manufactured wholesale and retail ice cream at the corner of Magnolia Avenue and Cherry Street, including private-label ice cream for Cas Walker and other grocery chains. (Jim and Margie Alexander.)

SWAN BROTHERS BAKERY. Charles and George Swan came to Knoxville from Chicago in the early 1880s and hired Louis Tauxe of Yens, Switzerland, as their chief baker. By the 1930s, they owned the 68,000-square-foot building at the corner of Magnolia Avenue and Bertrand Street. The building, just up from Park Place Condos, includes a gated parking lot and interior parking garage and would make excellent condos or offices. (Thompson Photo.)

Eight

THE FACES OF PARK CITY

Park City and the East Knoxville area have been home to a cast of colorful characters since before the Civil War. Francis Hodgson Burnett, author of *Vagabondia*, *The Secret Garden*, and *Little Lord Fauntleroy*, lived at Vagabondia Castle near Mabry Hill overlooking the river sometime around 1865. Her brother, Herbert Hodgson, a clock maker, operated his business at the corner of Mabry Street and Crozier Street, now Central Avenue.

Irene Hasley was walking by the old Camp Home for Friendless Women on McCalla Avenue in 1916. In a shack across the street, she heard the cries of the babies of these wayward women and knew she had to do something. She convinced Maj. Robert Camp to let her take over the old Florence Crittenton House at 2342 Woodbine Avenue, where she opened the Home for Friendless Babies. It operated there for several years before taking over a much larger building at 233 Cecil Street.

These are just some of the stories and faces of Park City. For some there are photographs. For others there are only memories. A book could probably be written about each one.

From Gen. Joseph A. Mabry to Cal Johnson, Fernando C. Beaman, and others, the faces and personalities of Park City, Mountain View, and Burlington are unique and interesting. This long, unbroken chain of colorful characters still exist and have only grown in number with each passing generation from such interesting folks as Bob Booker; Sara Moore Greene; Ace and Ted Ray Miller; Mose and Georgia Lee Lobetti; Bill Deatherage; Herman Wayland; Avon Rollins; and the Ashe sisters, Helen and Ellen, of Love's Kitchen. The list is much longer, but suffice to say Park City just keeps on producing interesting and important citizens who have played and will play a vital role in the history of Knoxville.

Park City has its fair share of eccentric folks in its past, but unlike some small cities, it does not hide them in a closet or lock them in a room upstairs. On the contrary, it brings them right into the parlor and sits them down to visit and share their thoughts and memories. Park City does not ask if there is someone eccentric in the family—just which side he is on.

BIG BROTHER'S MODEL A. Stewart Evans is shown here sitting in front of the family home at 3036 Magnolia Avenue. Brothers Tom and John are perched in the rumble seat hoping to go for a spin. The Beaman home and the Col. Moody home can be seen in the background. In later years, Stewart Evans would be instrumental in bringing the 1982 World's Fair to Knoxville—another Park Citian ahead of his time. (John Evans.)

ALL DRESSED AND READY TO GO. Childhood friends of Edythe Adcock Bell (not pictured) are seen here on one of the side streets that intersect with Washington Avenue. Notice the charming little outfits and hairstyles on the children—very typical of that era. (Edythe Adcock Bell.)

THE BEAMANS ON WHEELS. From left to right, daughters Libby and Jean, Mrs. Cora Beaman, and son Alvin are shown here in the front yard of their home on Magnolia Avenue. Even baby Alvin seems ready to roll as he is seen sitting on a tiny tricycle being steadied by his mother's loving hand. (Marge Beaman Jeffries.)

LITTLE GIRLS AND BABY DOLLS. The lovely front porch of the Beaman home on Magnolia was the perfect place for two little girls to play with their baby dolls. Pictured are two Beaman daughters, Margie (Jeffries) and Chickie (Charlotte Beaman Tate). Little-girl tea parties and playing dress up were some of their favorite things to do on this covered porch. (Marge Beaman Jeffries.)

SUNDAY MORNING BEST. This is a photograph of the Beaman family following Sunday church services. Everyone is all dressed up and looking forward to the Sunday luncheon that Mrs. Beaman always prepared after church. Clarence and Cora Beaman always invited anyone who wished to join them to come to their Magnolia Avenue home and share lunch with the family. (Marge Beaman Jeffries.)

THE DODSON FAMILY ON PATTON STREET. The C. C. Dotson family lived in this lovely Victorian home on Patton Street. This c. 1900 photograph shows many of the Dotson family members. Large homes such as this were abundant in Park City and were perfect to raise large families. C. C. Dotson was a well-known jeweler in Knoxville and owned a business in the downtown area. (Beck Center.)

HENRY HOPEWELL AND HIS DOG, SPOT. Henry Hopewell and his dog, Spot, pose in front of the Carnegie Library seated in his mule-drawn carriage. Hopewell was a familiar citizen throughout Park City, Mountain View, and Burlington. (Beck Center.)

JAMES BECK. James Garfield Beck and Ethel Benson Beck were African-American educators and entrepreneurs. James Beck came to Knoxville for school, graduating from Knoxville College in 1906. He taught at Austin High and was the first athletic director at Knoxville College. Beck was one of the chief organizers of the Knoxville Branch NAACP in 1919. He was a candidate for city council in 1951. (Beck Center.)

PEDALING IN PARK CITY. All children loved to go riding on their tricycles and bicycles when the weather permitted. Pictured here is a photograph of a little girl from Park City who is taking advantage of a lovely day to get some exercise on her little tricycle. (Beck Center.)

PICKELL GIRLS AND FRIENDS. In this picture are, from left to right, Edith Pickell, twins Eleanor and Helen Pickell, Virginia Bird, Jonathan Howes, Mary Mayne Wilson, Kathryn Bird, Carol Heflin, Jennings Bird, and Nancy Howes. The picture is dated "February 16, 1941, in front of the Pickells." The house still stands at 3037 East Fifth Avenue. (Margery Bensey/Edith Pickell Williams.)

SUMMER DAYS ON WOODBINE. Sue French and her younger sister, Ann, enjoy a spring day together in the front yard of their home at 2854 Woodbine Avenue. In the background is the house they would later move into at 2861 Woodbine. Like many of the homes in Park City, this one was designed for a growing family and offered more than 3,000 square feet of living space. (Becky French Brewer.)

POTTY TRAINING IN PARK CITY. It must have been a pretty day in Park City, as we see Jane Anne Parker's parents have decided to let her practice potty training outside. The building in the background is Park City Lowry School. It was located on Linden Avenue and had been the local high school until Knoxville High School was completed in 1910. (Jane Anne Parker.)

THE KIDS FROM LINDEN AVENUE. Posed in this photograph are Jim Sharp, Jane Ann Parker, and Tom Black Jr. Tom Black Sr. began a small snack business in the basement of his home on Linden Avenue. This cottage business developed into a huge corporation known as Tom's Snack Foods. The Tom Black Track at University of Tennessee is named in honor of Tom Black Sr. In later years, Tom Jr. assumed the family business. Jim Sharp became a pharmacist for Sharp's Drugs, the family business originally on Magnolia Avenue. (Jane Anne Parker.)

LIZA STOKLEY STONE AND FERN WAYLAND. Stone was secretary to city court judge Kelly for many years and rented apartments in her home at Milligan and East Fifth. Wayland's son, Herman, was elected Knox County sheriff by the largest margin for a Democratic candidate. Stone rented an apartment to a young man named Joe Fowler, who would later become Knoxville chief of police and then Knox County sheriff. Both ladies were influential in the Democratic Party. (Anne Wayland Lambert.)

MICKEY AND DITTO WAYLAND. Mickey Wayland and her brother, Herman Houston "Ditto" Wayland Jr., pose in front of Anne Wayland's little sports car. After serving as Miss Tennessee in 1959, Mickey and Ditto toured together as a singing act, playing to sell-out crowds wherever they performed. Ditto continued his career as a nightclub entertainer in Florida. Mickey is now retired and living in Hawaii. (Anne Wayland Lambert.)

FIVE OF THE WAYLAND BROTHERS. From left to right, Charles Jr., Benjamin, Herman, Clifford, and Richard (Dick) Wayland are pictured in front of their home on Castle Street in Park City. Yet to be born were Ted and Anne Wayland. Their mother, Ina Fern Wayland, enjoyed lining the boys up like stair steps and taking their picture. (Anne Wayland Lambert.)

A WAR HERO IS BORN. Infant Richard (Dick) Wayland is shown here in his wicker baby carriage, the fifth of six boys. He grew up to become a lieutenant in the Army Air Force and piloted a B-17 aircraft in World War II. He was awarded the Distinguished Air Medal and three oak leaf clusters. This little fellow grew up to become a real hero. (Anne Wayland Lambert.)

A WAR HERO IS BURIED. After flying nearly 100 successful missions over Germany in his B-17, Dick Wayland volunteered to fly a nurse to England. The small, war-torn plane he used began to disintegrate, and the tower told Dick to parachute just before landing. The nurse refused to jump and he refused to leave her. Both died, and he was buried temporarily in England. His father, Charles, who had been gravely ill, died December 23, 1947, 30 minutes after learning that Dick's body had arrived in Park City. A double funeral was held, and they were buried together at Woodlawn Cemetery on December 26, 1947. (Anne Wayland Lambert.)

BACKYARD THEATRE IN PARK CITY.
From left to right, schoolgirls Mary Costa, twins Eleanor Broome Pickell and Helen Woodward Pickell, and older sister Edith Gertrude Pickell are theatrically dressed for a backyard performance at the Pickell home at 3019 (now 3037) East Fifth Avenue c. 1939–1940. Mary Costa is an opera singer who retired in 1984 with 44 operas in her repertoire. Costa's voice is known around the world for her portrayal of Princess Aurora in the 1959 Disney animated film classic *Sleeping Beauty*. She also performed at the memorial service for President Kennedy at the request of First Lady Jacqueline Kennedy. (Helen Pickell Lobertini Schaich.)

EASTER SUNDAY. Faye Cleveland French and her three daughters, Sue (Sweat) (left), Becky (Brewer) (middle), and Ann (Pepper), are shown here. This photograph was taken in the early 1950s at the family home located at 2854 Woodbine Avenue. These little Easter outfits were hand-sewn by French for her daughters. She and Henry French were married for 52 years prior to her death in 1990. (Becky French Brewer.)

THE LEVY-LICHT HOME ON MAGNOLIA AVENUE. Richard Licht's grandmother, Jenny Samuel Levy, is seen here with her brothers in front of 2918 and 2922 Magnolia Avenue. They lived here from 1922 until 1948. Born in Knoxville, Jenny married Albert Levy, who was stationed at one of the three army camps around Knoxville during the Spanish-American War. One evening, he was invited to the Samuel home for dinner and met Jenny. (Richard M. Licht.)

ANNE WAYLAND LAMBERT. Anne Wayland, sister of Sheriff Herman Wayland, is shown here in the backyard of the Wayland home at 2812 Woodbine Avenue. This photograph was probably taken in the 1950s, before Anne married Walter Lambert, a well-known Knoxville chef and author. (Anne Wayland Lambert.)

PARK CITY'S OWN MISS TENNESSEE. Mickey Wayland, daughter of former Knox County sheriff Herman Wayland, is pictured here in Atlantic City at the Miss America pageant in 1959. She was first runner up in the year that Mary Ann Mobley was crowned Miss America. In the Miss Tennessee pageant, the first runner up that year was future actress Dixie Carter. The Wayland family lived on Woodbine Avenue. Just before leaving for Atlantic City, the neighbors got together and formed a jubilant send off for Mickey. She rounded the corner from East Fifth Avenue onto Woodbine and was met with bells, whistles, confetti, and placards pronouncing her as, "Our Next Miss America." This caused Mickey to cry, and before you knew it, every mom, dad and kid on the block was crying with her. (Anne Wayland Lambert.)

SHERIFF HERMAN WAYLAND. Herman Wayland was born in Park City and served in the Navy in World War II. In 1952, he rose to the rank of detective in the Knoxville Police Department. Elected sheriff in 1960, he is best known for the infamous "midnight liquor raid" he launched against every club in the city and county. This raid included previously protected private country clubs that had never experienced this sort of treatment. Perhaps that accounts for the fact that he was not re-elected in 1962. Herman and Jeri Goodwill Wayland had one child, Eddie, and Herman had two children, Herman H. Wayland Jr. (Ditto) and Marion (Mickey), from a previous marriage. The family lived at 2847 Woodbine Avenue. (Anne Wayland Lambert.)

BOYS AND DOGS IN PARK CITY. The Frye boys, Kenneth, J. W., and Glenn, children of Nelly Brooks and Joseph William Frye, are pictured in 1946 with their pet dog. The 11 Frye children grew up in Shieldstown between the 1920s and 1940s, and they lived at 2010 Islington Avenue and 1215 Linden Avenue. (Margery Bensey/J. W. Frye.)

WILLIAM HENRY FRENCH. William Henry French is shown here with his daughter, Becky French Brewer, in front of the family home at 2854 Woodbine Avenue. Mr. French worked for the Railway Express Agency located in the Southern Railroad Depot. He was also a homebuilder and built homes in Park City, Holston Hills, North Knoxville, and Old Central Avenue Pike. He was born in Jefferson County and married Faye Cleveland of Corryton, Tennessee. (Becky French Brewer.)

AT HOME ON MAGNOLIA. The Duncan family is shown here at the second home they owned in Park City. Pictured are George and Frances Duncan with their young son, Jerry. Notice the turreted porch on the home, the perfect place to sit and enjoy a summer evening reading the paper and drinking a glass of ice-cold tea. (Jerry Duncan.)

117

WAITING FOR THE PONY MAN. Patsy Falkner Scruggs and her little cousin from Alabama are pictured here purchasing ice cream. Many a child in Park City from the 1930s until the 1960s can recall Kay's Ice Cream and their charming pony carts and tinkling bells. Kay's plant and retail store were located at the southeast corner of Magnolia Avenue and Cherry Street. Pony carts were eventually replaced with shiny trucks playing children's melodies. (Jim and Margie Alexander.)

AN ITALIAN IMMIGRANT IN PARK CITY. At 18, Joseph Lobetti-Bodoni arrived in New York from Italy. Moving south to Coal Creek (now Lake City), Tennessee, he became a L&N Railroad baggage handler. He married Sheriff Lidge DeMarcus's daughter, Minnie, when she was 16. In Knoxville, he became a baggage master. He later worked for Holston National Bank as the building superintendent and knew a great deal about caves under downtown buildings. The Lobettis and their 10 children moved to Park City to 2701 East Fifth Avenue. (Robert Mose Lobetti.)

HARD WORK EQUALS SUCCESS.
This letter was written by future congressman John J. Duncan Sr. on January 21, 1940. He was a student at University of Tennessee and was employed at the Milner Hotel in downtown Knoxville when he sent this letter to his folks. Duncan, with nine siblings at home, arrived in Knoxville determined to work his way through college. The contents of this letter speak volumes. "It is a little hard to work all night on Wednesday, go to school until noon until Thursday, and back to work at three thirty the same day." (Lynn and Jimmy Duncan.)

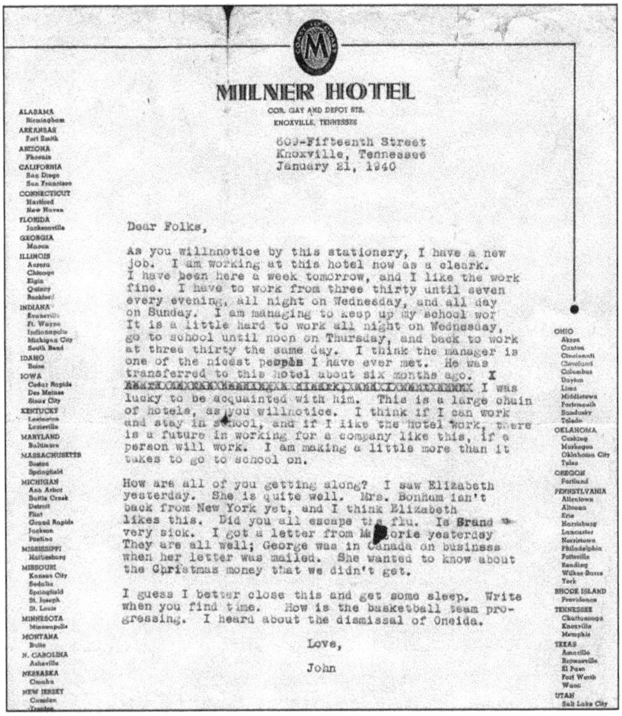

MILNER HOTEL
COR. GAY AND DEPOT STS.
KNOXVILLE, TENNESSEE

603-Fifteenth Street
Knoxville, Tennessee
January 21, 1940

Dear Folks,

As you will notice by this stationery, I have a new job. I am working at this hotel now as a cleark. I have been here a week tomorrow, and I like the work fine. I have to work from three thirty until seven every evening, all night on Wednesday, and all day on Sunday. I am managing to keep up my school work It is a little hard to work all night on Wednesday, go to school until noon on Thursday, and back to work at three thirty the same day. I think the manager is one of the nicest people I have ever met. He was transferred to this hotel about six months ago. I ＸＸＸＸＸＸＸＸＸＸＸＸＸＸ ＸＸＸＸＸＸＸＸＸＸＸ I was lucky to be acquainted with him. This is a large chain of hotels, as you will notice. I think if I can work and stay in school, and if I like the hotel work, there is a future in working for a company like this, if a person will work. I am making a little more than it takes to go to school on.

How are all of you getting along? I saw Elizabeth yesterday. She is quite well. Mrs. Bonham isn't back from New York yet, and I think Elizabeth likes this. Did you all escape the flu. Is Brand very sick. I got a letter from Marjorie yesterday They are all well; George was in Canada on business when her letter was mailed. She wanted to know about the Christmas money that we didn't get.

I guess I better close this and get some sleep. Write when you find time. How is the basketball team progressing. I heard about the dismissal of Oneida.

Love,

John

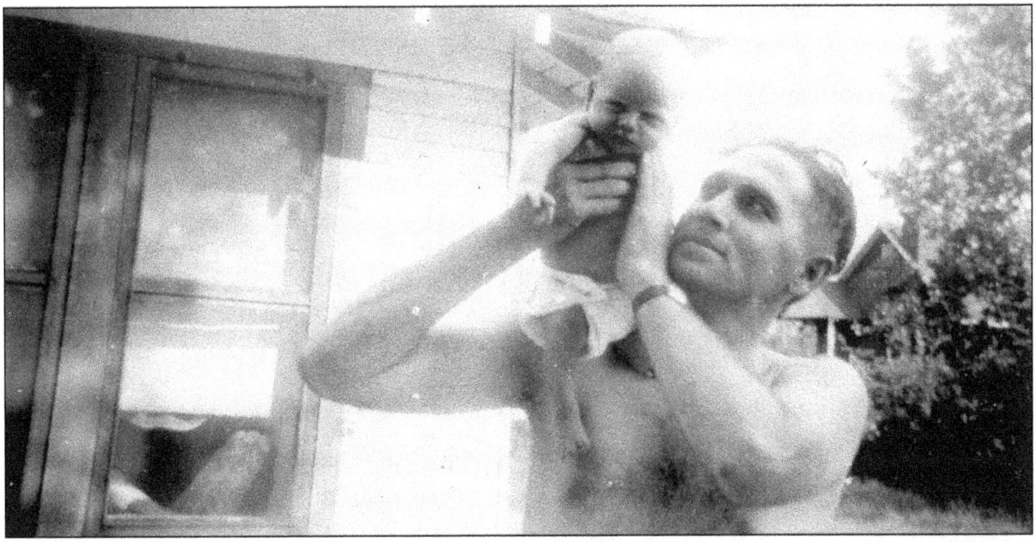

TWO FUTURE TENNESSEE CONGRESSMEN. John J. Duncan Sr. and his son John J. (Jimmy) Duncan Jr. are shown here in front of their home in the Veterans Village Project on McCalla Avenue (now Martin Luther King Jr. Boulevard) in Park City. John Duncan Sr. had arrived in Knoxville with a $25 scholarship check from Sears and Roebuck to attend the University of Tennessee. He served in the army from 1942 to 1945 and received his law degree from Cumberland University in 1947. Duncan was mayor of Knoxville from 1959 to 1965, when he ran for U.S. Congress from the 2nd District. A popular conservative, he served 12 terms until his death June 21, 1988. His son, Jimmy, pictured here as a baby, stepped in a ran for his father's seat in Congress that same year and, as of 2005, is in his ninth term. From humble beginnings, these two men rose to place of national importance. (Lynn and Jimmy Duncan.)

PLAYTIME IN PARK CITY. John J. (Jimmy) Duncan Jr. (seated on the scooter) and his unidentified friends play in front of his parent's home in the Veterans Village Project on McCalla Avenue. Many young families began climbing the ladder of success here. This apartment complex was razed for the construction of the present day Austin-East High School. As of 2005, U.S. Congressman Jimmy Duncan is serving his ninth term in office. (Lynn and Jimmy Duncan.)

LAND OF HIGH HORIZONS. Elizabeth Skaggs Bowman and her husband, E. L. Bowman, owned this home at 2358 Linden Avenue. They owned the Bowman Hat Company, located first in the Old City. In the 1950s, they moved the business to Bearden, where they named two streets Mohican Drive and Homberg Drive in honor of two popular hats. A member of the Appalachian Club at Elkmont in the Great Smoky Mountains, Mrs. Bowman was the author of the 1938 book *Land of High Horizons*, the first book written about the Smoky Mountains. She was active in historic preservation of Ramsey House, Fort Loudon, and the John Sevier home. (Jamie Rowe.)

YOUNG PALS IN PARK CITY. From left to right, George Tampas, unknown, John Cavalaris, Charlie Regas, Frank Regas, and Jim Cavalaris pose in this *c.* 1945 photograph. George would go on to run a liquor store in Burlington, John would become a dentist, Charlie and Frank would continue their father's restaurant, and Jim would work for NASA. John and Jim's father, Gus, owned the New York Café at Vine and Central. (Pete Psihogios.)

THE GUS PEROULAS HOME ON LINDEN AVENUE. This is the Peroulas house on Linden Avenue where Gus, Arthur, and Al Peroulas lived with their families until the 1960s, when they purchased three lots in West Hills from Wanda Moody's father. The family has lived together since they came to Knoxville. Here Gus's sister-in-law, Faye Kampas, holds Gus's daughter, Victoria Peroulas Pliagas. (Pete Psihogios.)

JAMES PSIHOGIOS VISITS GEORGE REGAS. James Psihogios, who ran the Atlanta Café on north Gay Street with Nick Passiakos, relaxes on George Regas's porch on the corner of Linden Avenue and Harrison Street. The Consin (Kotsianas) house is visible in the background. (Pete Psihogios.)

FAMILY PORTRAIT. James Psihogios came from Frangista, Greece, in 1919 to join his father Pereclies "Pete" Psihogios at the Central Café on Pack Square in Asheville, North Carolina. James married Fotine Kletchis in Vineni, Greece, in 1934 and brought her back in 1947 after World War II. Their son, George, co-owned the Garden Restaurant on Gay Street with George Consin (Kotsianas). Pete Psihogios was born in Knoxville in 1948 and went to work at the Y-12 nuclear facility in Oak Ridge. (Pete Psihogios.)

MARIKA PASSIAKOS AND NICK APOSTOLOU. Marika Passiakos and her grandson, Nick Apostolou, pose for a picture in front of the Passiakos house at 2767 Linden Avenue. (Pete Psihogios.)

AN AFTERNOON STROLL FOR MOM AND BABY. Nitsa Lampbros and John Lampbros lived in the 2400 block of Linden Avenue. John worked at the Gold Sun Restaurant on Market Square, now Gus's Restaurant on the northwest corner of the square. (Pete Psihogios.)

CATCH ME, DADDY. Pete Psihogios dares to jump off the porch into his father James's arms in this 1953 photograph at 2615 Linden Avenue. James arrived in this country from Greece, fell in love with East Tennessee and Park City, and decided to make this place his home. He was co-owner of the Atlanta Café, located in downtown Knoxville. (Pete Psihogios.)

PROUD PAPA IN PARK CITY. Arthur Aston is pictured holding his infant son, Arthur Jr., high above his head in front of the Aston Apartments at 2736 Magnolia Avenue. This photograph was made more than 70 years ago. Aston was well known for the quality of his construction, and this property still stands as a testament to his craftsmanship. (Barbara Aston-Wash.)

KIDS IN THE PARK. Barbara Aston-Wash, Arthur Aston Jr., and John Burnette enjoy a day of fun at Chilhowee Park. This area of the park, which is now known as the midway, was once a wonderful place to play. It had several pools and lovely gardens with hand-stacked rock walls. The Astons lived across the street at the corner of Linden and Beaman Street. (Barbara Aston-Wash.)

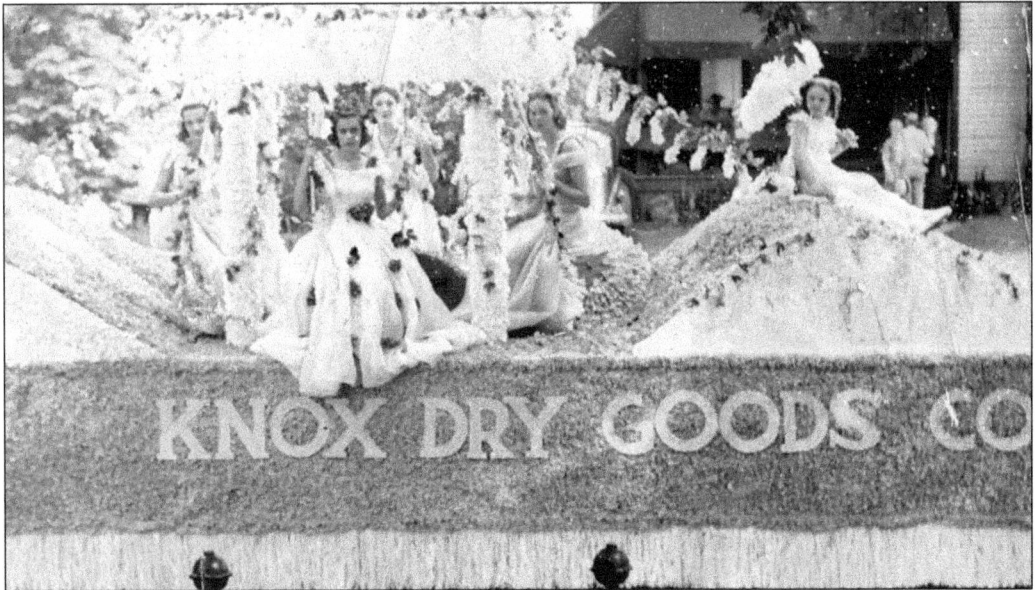

WILDFLOWER FESTIVAL FLOAT ON FIFTH AVENUE. In 1939, a young Barbara Aston-Wash sits atop the Knox Dry Goods Float for the Wildflower Festival Parade, the predecessor to the Dogwood Arts Festival. She holds a parasol to shade herself at the front of the float. Her uncle, Bunt Burnette, worked as a window display designer for Knox Dry Goods. He was responsible for decorating this beautiful float for the parade. (Barbara Aston-Wash.)

SAFELY HOME FROM WORLD WAR II. Evans brothers Dick, a B-17 pilot (at left, with his father in his lap); Tom, a B-25 pilot (center); Stewart, a B-24 pilot; and John, a B-24 navigator (seated in front), are pictured in May 1946 with their parents, W. E. and Helen Evans. While at Randolf Field in San Antonio, Texas, Stewart Evans took part and appears in the famous World War II movie *I Wanted Wings.* (John Evans.)

READY FOR A SUNDAY DRIVE. The Evans and Stewart families gather in front of the Evans home at 3036 Magnolia Avenue in 1921. From left to right are Gene Stewart Moore, Stewart Evans (in front of the rear tire), Bob Moore, unidentified, Grandpa Albert Stewart, Marion Moore, Grandma Stewart, and Helen Stewart-Evans holding Dick Evans. The Moores lived three blocks away at 2749 Linden Avenue. (John Evans.)

JULIUS WALKER AND THE BUDWEISER CLYDESDALES. Julius Walker, owner of Walker's Bar-B-Q at 3225 Magnolia Avenue, poses with the Budweiser Clydesdale horses on November 4, 1950, on Magnolia Avenue. (Charlie and Sue Walker.)

MEMORIAL DAY IN PARK CITY. Cora Goddard Beaman is the driver of the eight-passenger Studebaker on this Memorial Day outing in 1921 on Magnolia Avenue. The flowers and flags the children are holding were later placed on the graves of fallen soldiers at the National Cemetery. Patriotism was the order of the day throughout Knoxville on Memorial Day. (Marge Beaman Jeffries.)

EPILOGUE

If there is one thing that has become abundantly clear to the writers of this book, it is that Park City, Mountain View, and Burlington are making a noticeable comeback after years of neglect. The revitalization of downtown Knoxville has created a renewed interest in these long forgotten little cities, and a new surge of growth can be felt throughout the community.

Once-abandoned and neglected homes are being restored to their former glory all over this area known collectively as East Knoxville. People are reclaiming their real identity and proudly referring to themselves as Park City people once again. Homeowners are standing hand-in-hand and demanding better law enforcement and better codes enforcement throughout the area, and they are finally being heard. Neighborhood groups are beginning to join together and are in the fledgling stages of creating a Park City Town Hall, which will work under one roof with every citizen to help solve the problems facing the community. After years of silence, home and business owners in this diverse, multi-ethnic community realize that together they can speak with a much stronger voice—accomplishing what they have been unable to do as individuals. Park City has an almost equal population of whites and African Americans working together to establish unity and common community goals.

Everyone agrees that connectivity with downtown Knoxville is a positive thing. Park City has always been the main core of support for the retail stores, restaurants, theaters, and other businesses in downtown Knoxville. Residents need them, and they need residents, and that is a good thing for every one concerned with the growth and prosperity of this great city.

The authors hope that this book will help shed new light on a long-forgotten and truly beautiful area of this city. Until Park City and Mountain View were annexed in 1917, they were thriving, independent municipalities. We hope this book will encourage residents of historic Park City, Mountain View, and Burlington to never again allow themselves to become lost, neglected, or abandoned. If nothing else, may this book remind everyone that Park City is a truly historic community and should be cared for and treasured for future generations.

The groundwork has already begun. Property in some pocket neighborhoods has tripled in value over the past few years. New residents and businesses are needed in Park City and will be welcomed with open arms.

Visit us at
arcadiapublishing.com